CHIPLEY MCQUEEN THORNTON

POINT-TO-POINT
PREACHING

Point-to-Point Preaching

Copyright © 2023 by Chipley McQueen Thornton

Published by G3 Press
4979 GA-5
Douglasville, GA 30135
www.G3Min.org

All rights reserved. No part of this publication may be reproduced, stored in a retrieval system, or transmitted in any form by any means, electronic, mechanical, photocopy, recording, or otherwise, without prior permission of the publisher, except as provided for by USA copyright law.

Scripture quotations are from the ESV® Bible (*The Holy Bible, English Standard Version*®), copyright © 2001 by Crossway, a publishing ministry of Good News Publishers. Used by permission. All rights reserved. All emphases in Scripture quotations have been added by the author.

Printed in the United States of America by Graphic Response, Atlanta, GA

ISBN: 978-1-959908-99-9

Cover Design: Joe Zarate

Contents

Preface i

Introduction 1

The Author's Intent 17

    1   If God Didn't Mean What He Said, Then Why Didn't He Say What He Meant? 19

    2   Correcting a Crisis 27

    3   Unmasking Satan's Motive 33

    4   Why Didn't You Preach What *I* Wrote? 43

Context 49

    5   Context, Context, Context 51

    6   Book Context 57

    7   Sectional Context and "If My People..." Theology 63

    8   Immediate Context and "Fallen Away from Grace..." 69

Syntax 75

    9   The Impact of Syntax 77

    10   Does God Care About Paragraph Syntax? 83

    11   Syntax in Psalm 1 91

| 12 | Does Jesus Care About Syntax? | 99 |
| 13 | Word Meaning Matters | 105 |

Interpretation ... 111

14	Head Coverings and Cultural Norms	113
15	Scripture Interprets Scripture	123
16	Is Christ in Every Text?	131
17	Is a Text Pregnant with Meanings?	139
18	Closing the Gate on Allegory	149
19	Bridging the Gap Between *Then* and *Now*	157
20	"See Spot Run" & the Sufficiency of Scripture	163
21	The Greatest Problem in Preaching Today	169
22	The Danger of Exemplarist Preaching	177
23	The Danger of Atomistic Preaching	185
24	The Danger of Biographical Sermons	193

Application ... 197

25	Point-to-Point Application	199
26	Abstraction	205
27	Extrapolation	211
28	Principlization	217
29	Reaching from the Grave	225

Homiletics 231

30	Sermon Steps 233
31	Drafting A Sermon Outline 241
32	Thinking Through the Entire Sermon 247
33	Should I Have Heretics in My Home? 253
34	Power Struggles in the Congregation 261
35	How Many Minutes Should a Sermon Last? 269
36	Sermon Length and the Sufficiency of Scripture 275
37	Chasing the Wrong Rabbits 281
38	Preaching with Spirit-Power 289
39	Things (on Preaching) They Didn't Tell Me in Seminary 295

Preface

This book originated from a series of lectures on preaching I've delivered in several parts of the world: the United States, Ecuador, Senegal, Nigeria, and France. Admittedly, it follows closely both the flow and the principles set forth by Walter C. Kaiser, Jr. in *Toward an Exegetical Theology*.[1] His is one of the best books ever written on the subject of Christian preaching. In 2016, I corresponded with Dr. Kaiser before preparing those lectures, and he offered some insightful advice; namely, use lots of illustrations and sermon samples. He has always been kind to me.

I studied preaching under Al Fasol. The homiletical sections, naturally, have much carry-over from Dr. Fasol's

---

[1] Walter C. Kaiser, Jr., *Toward an Exegetical Theology* (Grand Rapids: Baker Book House, 1981). We recognize that, later in his ministry, Kaiser drifted toward egalitarianism. While we cannot follow him there, we still respect his sound hermeneutical and homiletical principles as a valuable contribution to Christ's Kingdom. We can glean those principles from him without following him into egalitarianism. Indeed, we suggest that if you follow his hermeneutical principles, it will lead, rather, to a healthy biblical view of complementarianism. Much of what follows are principles derived from Kaiser's work. I have spoken with him once and corresponded with him several times about my teaching those principles around the world. He has always been gracious to me.

lectures and textbook, *Steps to the Sermon*.[2] Even where my thoughts might be unique, his influence shaped them. Dr. Fasol, too, was always kind and gracious to me.

I gave them both credit throughout the book, but if I inadvertently neglected to do so somewhere, the idea likely originated not with me, but with one of them. I am grateful for them both.

---

[2] H.C. Brown, Jr., H. Gordon Clinard, Jesse J. Northcutt, and Al Fasol, *Steps to the Sermon: An Eight-Step Plan for Preaching with Confidence* (Nashville, TN: Broadman & Holman Publishers, 1996).

Introduction

"Do you want me to lie to you, or do you want me to tell you the truth?" a friend of mine often asks. We all know the answer to that question. We want the truth. The truth is this: Christian preaching today, largely, is weak and powerless. Why is this? Oh, we could decry all the awful gimmicks that masquerade as Christian preaching. That certainly makes us feel better, but it really doesn't solve anything. I'd like to offer a different approach. Sometimes, if we understand how the problem developed, we can see more clearly how to treat it. In what follows, let's: (1) diagnose the *problem*; (2) describe the *symptoms*; and then, (3) discuss the proven *solution*.

Diagnosing the Problem

In a sentence, the problem is this: Christian preaching has lost its prophetic voice.

One of the single greatest human acts on earth—if not the greatest—is Christian preaching. After all, God sent his Son to this planet as a preacher. The Apostle Paul declares Christian preaching as God's designed means (1) to redeem his elect children (Rom 10:17) and (2) to translate them from Satan's world of darkness into Christ's Kingdom of light (Col 1:13). Preaching, by its nature and content, was designed to be powerful and penetrating. Yet, today we find the discipline of preaching, largely, impotent.

The problem is being exacerbated, often unwittingly, by a new generation of preachers. They are attempting to correct the problem in new ways rather than trusting in the old one (which we'll discuss below). They've only made matters worse: "woke" hermeneutics (the latest rage) in America, the "health, wealth, and prosperity" preaching in Africa, moralism in other parts of the world, counseling-centered hermeneutics, man-centered preaching, entertainment-driven preaching, "disguised" preaching, or even no preaching at all. Try as they might, they've only served to deepen the problem. Why? Because all their methodologies, whether they realize it or not, are the same at the most fundamental level: an age-old attempt to demean or deny the biblical author's original intent in Scripture texts. This began with Satan's opening line in Scripture, "Did God really say . . ." (Gen 3:1)?

This new generation of preachers would never admit they demean or deny the sufficiency of Scripture. Most aren't even aware they do. Yet, their practices betray their proclamations. They inherently deny the sufficiency of Scripture, whether they admit it or not. Once this happens, as Martin Luther warns us, Scripture perishes, and

Introduction

good theologians are no longer produced.[1] History confirms this and also suggests it normally requires a reformation or a revolution (or both) to correct it. Indeed, when Scripture loses its prophetic voice, we have a serious problem.

Describing the Symptoms

The chief symptom is this: *The world system has influenced the discipline of preaching moreso than the Word of God.* However, this primary symptom slings out all kinds of other symptoms. For instance, the preaching of our times is pathetic and powerless because it's engineered by man, emphasizes man, and seeks to entertain men. God is but an afterthought (if he's thought of at all). To cite an example, the latest fad is to show secular movies in lieu of a sermon, and then offer a spiritual soliloquy once the movie ends. One pastor recently assuaged any concerns this might provoke: "We're going to give you the Word of God," he assured us, "We're just going to disguise it a little bit." Never mind that Paul said, "I am not ashamed of the gospel" (Rom 1:16). You even can purchase pre-packaged "movie-kits," replete with the full movie, spliced clips, the

---

[1] Martin Luther, *Answer to the Hyperchristian, Hyperspiritual, and Hyper-learned Book by Goat Emser in Leipzig—Including Some Thoughts Regarding His Companion, the Fool Murner, 1521*, in *Luther's Works*, ed. Helmut T. Lehmann, vol. 39 (Philadelphia: Fortress, 1970), 178.

sermon transcripts, graphic designs, sermon outlines for the audience, bulletins, worship set lists, and (let's not forget) the limited license agreement (under the U.S. Copyright Act). In 2022, the price was $180.00: no shipping; all downloadable. Plagiarism is not denounced. Quite the opposite. It is designed, marketed, packaged, and sold for profit. No one even blushes about it anymore. Worse, the subject matter of the messages is shallow and unprophetic. It lacks biblical authority. We grant it is entertaining, but we deny it constitutes biblical preaching. It is impotent.

Yet, for students of history, this is not surprising. It is par for the course.

We might think the discipline of preaching has a long and distinguished history. Sadly, apart from a few glorious bright spots, the discipline of preaching has been ridiculed and uncelebrated. From the first recorded preacher of righteousness—Noah (no one outside his family listened to him)—to the Lord Jesus Christ himself (they murdered him) and beyond, Satan's world has belittled, berated, and beheaded gospel preachers. The irony is this: the very entity the discipline of preaching was designed to help—the wicked world system—ended up infiltrating and corrupting the discipline from the inside. It's the Trojan horse strategy. Of course, God always casts a line of faithful preachers for the sake of his elect remnant, and he always will. The rest, though, were too influenced by

Introduction

the world system to speak against it. Instead, they tried their best to amalgamate the Word of God with the ways of the world. For example, Isaiah tells us his contemporaries were filled with worldliness (Is 28:7); Jeremiah says his contemporaries were filled with carnality, adultery, and plagiarism (Jer 23:14, 20); the Lord Jesus chastises his contemporaries for, among other things, devouring widows' houses (Lk 20:47); the Apostle Paul informs us his contemporaries were greedy for dishonest gain (Tit 1:11); and, the Apostle Peter thundered that his contemporaries had eyes filled with adultery, hearts trained in greed, and voracious appetites for sin (2 Pet 2:14). They were not talking about the general populace, mind you. They were talking about the preachers. Yes, the reality is, apart from a few bright spots in human history, the world system has driven the discipline of preaching moreso than the Word of God.

Preachers are famous for playing "loosey-goosey" with God's Holy Word. Stoic preachers (ca. 333 BC) began to delve into allegory to synthesize ancient religious traditions with their worldly society.[2] Philo advanced these

---

[2] Marsha L. Colish, *The Stoic Tradition from Antiquity to the Early Middle Ages* (Leiden: E.J. Brill, 1985), 22-60; see also, J. Julius Scott, Jr., "Allegory," in *Tyndale Bible Dictionary*, ed. Walter A. Elwell and Philip W. Comfort (Wheaton: Tyndale, 2001), 29-30; Robert W. Bernard, "The Hermeneutics of the Early Church Fathers," in *Biblical Hermeneutics*, ed. Bruce Corley, Steve W. Lemke, and Grant I. Lovejoy, 2nd ed. (Nashville: Broadman and Holmon, 2002), 91-92; James D. Smart, *The Interpretation of Scripture* (Philadelphia: Westminster, 1961), 179-80.

allegorical tendencies in the first century (here we go again) to present his Jewish heritage as palatable to a sophisticated, but pagan, Greek society.[3] He suggested every text has two meanings: (1) a literal one and (2) a hidden one.[4] Pandora's box to polyvalent meanings was now cracked. The Apostles offered one of those few bright spots as they returned to scriptural authority rather than human ingenuity, and the world was turned upside down for Christ. Origen (third century), however, fell into allegorism (once again) to present the ancient text as relevant to his worldly audience.[5] He famously engineered the three-fold sense of Scripture texts: (1) the literal sense; (2) the moral sense; and, (3) the spiritual sense.[6] Another brief bright spot came in the fourth century when the Antiochene School—led by John Chrysostom among

---

[3] Anthony Thiselton, *New Horizons in Hermeneutics* (Grand Rapids: Zondervan, 1992), 160; see also, Samuel Sandmel, *Philo of Alexandria: An Introduction* (Oxford: Oxford University Press, 1979), 28; Erwin Goodenough, *An Introduction to Philo* (New Haven: Yale University Press, 1940), 124; Peder Borgen, *Philo of Alegandria: An Exegete for His Time* (Leiden: Brill, 1997), 9-13; Harry A. Wolfson, *Philo* (Cambridge, MA: Harvard University Press, 1947), 1:115-16, 138.

[4] See Wolfson, *Philo*, 1:115.

[5] Karen Jo Torjesen, *Hermeutical Procedure and Theological Method in Origen's Exegesis* (Berlin: Walter de Gruyter, 1986), 23-26, 130-30; David Dockery, *Biblical Interpretation Then and Now: Contemporary Hermeneutics in the Light of the Early Church* (Grand Rapids: Baker 1992), 96; Thiselton, *New Horizons*, 167-73.

[6] Harry A. Wolfson, *The Philosophy of the Church Fathers: Faith, Trinity, Incarnation*, vol. 1 (Cambridge: MA: Harvard University Press, 1956), 57-65 offers a good, detailed analysis on the subject.

Introduction

others—returned to the literal meaning of Scripture, but it was only a brief glow. Augustine (late fourth, early fifth century) arose to introduce not a three-fold sense in Scripture, but a four-fold sense: (1) historical; (2) aetiological; (3) analogical; and (4) allegorical.[7] Every text was now "pregnant" with meanings, and this notion descended down to the medieval period in what became formalized as the Quadriga. The Reformation, a bright and glorious era, returned to the literal meaning, but it was shortlived. The Reformation gave way to modernity (or, higher criticism), which (once again) sought to find common ground between the text and the reader (effectively, the "world"). To do so, it deconstructed the author's original intent, thus shifting authority from the author to the reader. Wilhelm Dilthey (1822-1911), for instance, stated, "We can understand an author better than he understood himself. Kant was the first to express this."[8] With the author "out of the way," the path was paved to run headlong into full-blown postmodernism. That is, a Scripture text (or any text, for that matter) no longer means what the original author intended it to mean. It means what each

---

[7] Dockery, *Biblical Interpretation*, 145; see also, Robert McNally, *The Bible in the Early Middle Ages* (Westminster: Newman, 1959), 54; Alistair McGrath, *Historical Theology: An Introduction to the History of Christian Thought* (Oxford: Blackwell, 1988), 144–46.

[8] Wilhelm Dilthey, *Hermeneutics and the Study of History*, trans. Rudolf A. Makkreel, ed. Rudolf A. Makkreel and Frithjof Rodi (Princeton, NJ: Princeton University Press, 1966), 232.

individual reader wills it to mean. Pandora's box to polyvalent meanings is now wide open. There are as many meanings as there are readers. This is the age in which we find ourselves, and it is a very dangerous age, indeed.

My intention heretofore was to show you how the *symptoms* emerged and developed. Next, let me slow down for a moment and focus on more recent history. It will be evident how it led to our present, terrible condition.

In 1967, E. D. Hirsch, Jr. tried to stop the insanity of higher criticism by restoring the original author to his rightful place of authority. In his book, *Validity in Interpretation*, he rightly separated the author's original "meaning" from any future "significance" of that meaning.[9] Hans-George Gadamer, in 1975, responded with a book entitled, *Truth and Method*, which blended (yet again) the horizon of the text and the horizon of the reader (effectively, the "world") in what he called the "fusion of

---

[9] E. D. Hirsch, Jr., *Validity in Interpretation* (London: Yale University Press, 1967). In an unnecessary concession, Hirsch later "walked back" his view in *Aims of Interpretation* (Chicago: University of Chicago press, 1976), 79–80. He enlarged "meaning" to "simply meaning-for-an-interpreter." Along with Kaiser, "The Current Crisis in Exegesis and the Apostolic Use of Deuteronomy 25:4 in 1 Corinthians 9:8-10," *JETS* 21 (1978): 4, we must "applaud Hirsch for his earlier distinction between 'meaning' and 'significance,'" but not "follow his most recent concession and thereby abandon the principle that 'meaning' is a return to what the author intended to say by his use of words in a particular text."

Introduction

horizons."[10] That fusion, he said, is where meaning can be found. In reality, it was a "*confusion*" of text and worldly influence.

Yet, the seeds Hirsch had sown began to bear a little fruit in the realm of Christian preaching. In 1980, Haddon Robinson published a book, *Biblical Preaching*, which was predicated upon determining the biblical author's "Big Idea" in each thought-unit.[11] Nothing like that had been seen in recent times. In 1981, Walter Kaiser, Jr. released a monumental book on Christian preaching, *Toward an Exegetical Theology*, which—coupled with Haddon Robinson's book—ignited a renewed interest in the biblical author's intent and in expository preaching.[12] Kaiser declared a "crisis in exegetical theology,"[13] and issued a clarion call to return to the single, verbal meaning of the biblical author to correct that crisis.

As I entered seminary studies in 1999, others had picked up the baton, and a host of fascinating preaching books had begun to take root. The trend became, let the preaching-text be the entering point to preach the whole Bible in every sermon. For example, in 1988, Sidney

---

[10] Hans-George Gadamer, *Truth and Method*, trans. J. Weinsheimer and D. G. Marshall, 2nd rev ed. (New York: Crossroad, 1989).

[11] Haddon Robinson, *Biblical Preaching: The Development and Delivery of Expository Messages* (Grand Rapids: Baker Book House, 1980).

[12] Walter C. Kaiser, Jr., *Toward an Exegetical Theology: Biblical Exegesis for Preaching and Teaching* (Grand Rapids: Baker Book House, 1981).

[13] Kaiser, *Toward an Exegetical Theology*, 17.

Greidanus published, *Modern Preacher and the Ancient Text*, which emphasized placing the preaching-text within the flow of redemptive history (or, the redemptive-historial metanarrative of Scripture).[14] In 1994, Bryan Chapell published *Christ-Centered Preaching*.[15] It sought to find the "fallen condition focus" in a text, and then show how Christ redeemed that fallen condition. In 2006, Graeme Goldsworthy published *Preaching the Whole Bible as Christian Scripture*, which overlays each preaching-text with the gospel in order to find Christ in every text.[16] Each of these books was helpful in its own right. They gave good credence to the biblical author's intent, but each also inherently brought an external analytical tool into the interpretive process: Greidanus read the text through the external grid of redemptive history; Chapell read the text through the external grid of the "fallen condition focus;" and Goldsworthy read the text through the external grid of the gospel. Each of these read the Bible backward, not forward, and in doing so, lost some of the uniqueness of

---

[14] Sidney Greidanus, *The Modern Preacher and the Ancient Text* (Grand Rapids: Eerdmans, 1988). He also published others like, *Preaching Christ from the Old Testament* (Grand Rapids: Eerdmans, 1999) and *Preaching Christ from Genesis: Foundations for Expository Preaching* (Grand Rapids: Eerdmans, 2007).

[15] Bryan Chapell, *Christ-Centered Preaching: Redeeming the Expository Sermon* (Grand Rapids: Baker Book House, 1994).

[16] Graeme Goldsworthy, *Preaching the Whole Bible as Christian Scripture: The Application of Biblical Theology to Expositional Preaching* (Grand Rapids: Eerdmans, 2000) and later, *Gospel-Centered Hermeneutics* (Nottingham: Intervarsity, 2006).

each preaching-text along the way. Every sermon ended up sounding the same, and a new generation of antsy preachers soon tired of the monotony. To escape it, they ran to other lovers (like man-engineered sermon kits), or else they returned to their old lover, allegorism, to "spice it up" a bit.

Nevertheless, I appreciated the Christ-centered approach of Greidanus, Chapell, etc., because I agreed with that Christ-centered worldview. Yet, they set a somewhat dangerous precedent. What happens when the external tool or worldview changes, and we *don't* agree with it? What happens when critical race theory and intersectionality (CRT/I) becomes an analytical tool? For instance, CRT/I sees every text as containing not a "fallen condition focus" (like Chapell), but rather an "oppresser vs. oppressed focus" that Christ must rescue. No longer is the worldview "the spiritually saved world" vs. "the spiritually lost world." Rather, it became "the physically/emotionally/financially oppressive world system" vs. "the physically/emotionally/financially oppressed world." Sometimes, you might have to strain to find it, which is precisely where the corruption of verbal meaning begins. The argument now is being made, for example, that since Zaccheus made financial reparations to those he had oppressed, then every Christian must make financial reparations to anyone who feels oppressed in their society—

whether they had anything to do with the oppression or not.

When we stop to consider, "What is driving all this?," the only common thread to all these symptoms is that the world system has driven Christian preaching moreso than the Word of God. From allegorical tendences in ancient times to "at the movies" sermon kits or race-centered hermeneutics in modern times, the motivating factor always is the same: an innate desire to engage the culture, to accommodate the culture, to synthesize the culture, and ultimately, to submit to the secular culture. Simply put, an innate desire to be "relevant" in the secular world. May I suggest an alternative approach?

Discussing the Solution

I have a much simpler solution: *Protect, preserve, and proclaim the biblical author's single intent in every thought-unit of Holy Scripture: nothing more; nothing less.*

Rather than attempting to make Holy Scripture "relevant" to Satan's world system and those in it, let Holy Scripture "correct," "change," or "condemn" it. I call it "point-to-point preaching." It doesn't attempt to preach the whole Bible in every sermon (though it does respect subsequent revelation). It doesn't attempt to accumulate dozens of proof-texts to "support" the preaching-text (that, on its face, inherently denies the sufficiency of

Introduction

Scripture). It doesn't try to aid the text to make it sound relevant (Scripture, by its God-breathed nature, *is* relevant). It certainly doesn't try to inject into the text certain external cultural accommodations, pet doctrines, personal agendas, secular ideologies, or clever allegories. It simply unleashes the power of the biblical author's single meaning into Satan's domain, and watches as the Holy Spirit convicts the world of sin and righteousness and judgment (Jn 16:8). Do this consistently, and what emerges—organically, not self-imposed—is the beautiful unveiling of the promise-plan of God which finds its perfect fulfillment in Christ. This happens as the uniqueness of individual Scripture texts are expounded consistently and applied correctly.

It's nothing new at all. It's a return to the old way; to the Protestant Reformers' way, the apostles' way, Jesus's way; the OT prophets' way; the only way that has ever worked: the fierce and unyielding commitment to the biblical author's single meaning in Scripture texts, despite what the culture says. All of the bright spots in the history of preaching, fundamentally, have been founded upon that. You can hear it in Jesus's most famous sermon, the Sermon on the Mount: "You have heard that it was said . . . But I say to you . . ." (Matt 5:21-22, 27-28, etc.). He was fixing their attention on the biblical author's original intent. You can hear it in the apostles' messages. When they engaged in serious exegesis of the OT, they always preserved the biblical writer's intended meaning.[17] The Protestant Reformers, Luther and Calvin, called it the "literal meaning," or "natural sense." But call it what you will—the big idea, the central idea, the single meaning, the verbal meaning, the author's intent, the author's willed meaning—it's all the same: preaching predicated on the biblical author's single meaning will find its prophetic voice and will speak into Satan's domain with prophetic power. Why? Because it is fiercely committed to the single meaning God-breathed Scripture texts.

John Stott wrote a wonderful book on preaching called, *Between Two Worlds*.[18] He spoke of bridging the gap between the (1) the ancient world and (2) the modern world. Yet, there are two other worlds Christian preaching must consider: (1) Satan's world (or kingdom) and (2) Christ's world (or Kingdom). Why are we so concerned with being relevant in Satan's world anyway? Why do we want a "seat at his table?" Why do we want a "voice in his sinful world system?" I understand the evangelistic appeal to reach Satan's deceived human subjects with Christ. We all feel that urgency. Yet, where are the men of God who will stand in Christ's Kingdom, proclaim his pure excellencies to Satan's world, and trust his Word will accomplish its intended purpose? Some will be hardened and

---

[17] Kaiser, Jr., *Toward an Exegetical Theology*, 57.
[18] John Stott, *Between Two Worlds* (Grand Rapids: William B. Eerdmans Publishing Co., 1982).

Introduction

cast into the lake of fire by it, to be certain (1 Pet 2:8b). Yet, others will be changed and gloriously translated into Christ's Kingdom (Col 1:13). But why would we ever plunge ourselves into Satan's world system and allow it to drive the method and message of our Christian preaching?

Is Holy Scripture sufficient to call out sinners from Satan's kingdom, destroy the antichrist, and make way for Christ's glorious appearing? Or, must we aid Holy Scripture by synthesizing it with secular culture to make it more palatable for them accept?

Point-to-point preaching rests on the former, not the latter. Indeed, Holy Scripture—proclaimed and declared—has sufficient power to impact Satan's kingdom without allegories or accommodations to Satan's world. Let the Christian preacher stand squarely in Christ's kingdom; let the Christian preacher protect, preserve, and proclaim the single meaning which God breathed-out to each biblical author in each thought-unit; let the Christian preacher declare that single meaning into Satan's domain; and let the Christian preacher sleep well as the Holy Spirit empowers it to accomplish Scripture's designed purpose.

Yes, Christian preaching has lost its prophetic voice. What follows calls Christian preachers to find their prophetic voice again, and it shows them how. That is what this book is about.

The Author's Intent

1

If God Didn't Mean What He Said, Then Why Didn't He Say What He Meant?

Upon hearing a whimsical sermon, the little boy asked, "If God didn't mean what He said, then why didn't He say what He meant?" A simple question, but it speaks to the heart of the sufficiency of Scripture, doesn't it? Consider ancient church father, Origen, and his explanation of the Good Samaritan:

> The traveler (Adam) journeys from Jerusalem (heaven) to Jericho (the world) and is assaulted by robbers (the devil and his helpers). The priest (the law) and the Levite (the prophets) pass by without aiding the fallen Adam, but the Samaritan (Christ) stops to help him, sets him on his breast (Christ's body) and brings him to an inn (the church), giving the innkeeper two denarii (the Father and the Son),

and promising to come back (Christ's second coming).¹

Is *that* actually what God is saying? The great Protestant Reformer, Martin Luther, didn't think so:

> That is why Origen received his due reward a long time ago when his books were prohibited, for he relied too much on this same spiritual meaning, which was unnecessary, and he let the necessary literal meaning go. When this happens Scripture perishes and really good theologians are no longer produced. Only the true and principal meaning which is provided in the letters can produce good theologians.²

Sadly, ours is a day of allegorists, many of whom don't even recognize they hold that infamous title. The same principles Origen used are being repackaged in our day, often by those who in theory reject the allegorical method. Luther was correct: "When this happens Scripture perishes," and that has disastrous implications: flawed soteriology, flawed ecclesiology, flawed theology, flawed responses to society's groanings, and more. Such allegorical vainjanglings today are—to borrow Kaiser's phrase—the

---

¹ Greidanus, *The Modern Preacher and the Ancient Text*, 159-60.
² Luther, *Answer to the Hyperchristian, Hyperspiritual, and Hyperlearned*, 178.

seedbed for tomorrow's heresies.³ Only one solution exists to the present crisis: A return to the sufficiency of Scripture, which means a return to expository preaching.

God Says what He Means

God breathed-out Scripture (2 Tim 3:16). It's one thing to acknowledge that fact. It's quite another to practice it in preaching. Think it through: If the Scripture writings (*graphe*) are God-breathed (2 Tim 3:16), then the actual words and their arrangement (syntax) must be examined carefully within their original historical context. We call this "exegesis" (that is, "to lead out of"). Our single aim must be to draw-out the pure meaning of the actual words (*graphe*) as God revealed them through His human authors. More specifically, exegesis seeks to:

> [I]identify the single truth-intention of individual phrases, clauses, and sentences as they make up the thought of paragraphs, sections, and, ultimately, entire books... exegesis may be understood in this work to be the *practice* of and the set of *procedures* for discovering the author's intended meaning.⁴

---

[3] Walter C. Kaiser, Jr., *Preaching and Teaching from the Old Testament* (Grand Rapids: Baker, 2003), 26.

[4] Kaiser, *Toward an Exegetical Theology*, 47.

Preaching rooted in sound exegesis "exposes" God's Word to men. We hear the term "expository preaching" often, but few know what it means; even less actually practice it. Walt Kaiser offers the most specific and comprehensive definition I've found:

> [T]hat method of proclaiming the Scriptures that takes as a minimum one paragraph of Biblical text (in prose narrative or its equivalent in other literary genre) and derives from the text both the shape (i.e., the main points and subpoints of the sermon) and the content (i.e., the substance, ideas, and principles) of the message itself.[5]

Simply put, expository preaching preserves, protects, and proclaims the biblical author's single meaning in each preaching-text. This method—at one and the same time—preserves, protects, and proclaims both the authority and the sufficiency of God's Scripture. It conveys, "God says what He means."

God Means What He Says

Not only does God say what He means, He means what He says. Many of our present-day problems will be

---

[5] Walter C. Kaiser, Jr., "The Crisis in Expository Preaching Today," *Preaching* (Sep-Oct 1995): 4.

If God Didn't Mean What He Said, Then Why Didn't He Say What He Meant?

corrected when we commit to expository preaching. Some God-honoring benefits will be:

1. *Expository preaching will glorify God.* God chose to reveal Himself to us in writing. If we truly treasure His Word, we will study it (2 Tim 2:15), rightly divide it (2 Tim 2:15), and proclaim it (2 Tim 4:2). When we accurately proclaim what the King has written, we glorify His Majesty. The proper proclamation of God's Word is the engine that drives our worship.

2. *Expository preaching will fulfill the Great Commission.* Expository preaching is one of the best means in fulfilling the Great Commission (Matt 28:19-20). It offers the greatest width, breadth, and depth of what God has revealed to mankind about Himself. It is the most faithful means of presenting *"everyone mature in Christ"* (Col. 1:28).

3. *Expository preaching will correct flawed soteriology.* Preach paragraph-by-paragraph through the book of Romans. Scripture will begin to correct decades of defective understandings regarding salvation *and* effectually call-out individuals unto salvation.

4. *Expository preaching will correct flawed ecclesiology.* Preach expositionally through texts regarding church polity, church structure, church membership, etc. Members will begin to ask beautiful questions like, "Why do we do it this way?" and, "Why aren't we do it the Scripture-way?" Correct ecclesiology will produce deeper, stronger disciples.

5. *Expository preaching will correct flawed theology.* Preach expositionally through books of the Bible. Watch how it sharpens, refines, and deepens everyone's theology (including yours!). A steady diet of exposition will bring everyone in concert with God's revealed will.

6. *Expository preaching will hold pastors accountable.* Every true man of God wants to stand before God and say with Paul, "I did not shrink from declaring . . . the whole counsel of God" (Acts 20:27). There is but one way to make that declaration stick: Expository preaching. It doesn't allow you to skip difficult or uncomfortable passages.

7. *Expository preaching will speak to current events.* God's Word has abiding relevance: It is living and active and discerns the intentions of all of mankind's heart (Heb 4:12). It exposes the world's actions, reactions, and motives. It exposes the world's elementary principles (Col 2:8) and destroys every lofty opinion it raises against the knowledge of God (2 Cor 10:5). Further, it provides comforting answers to a society that groans under sin's curse.

Closing Appeal

Faithful expository preaching fundamentally changed the church and society during the Protestant Reformation (education, laws, architecture, art, etc.), and it has the capacity to do so again today. It starts with purity in the

If God Didn't Mean What He Said, Then Why Didn't He Say What He Meant?

pulpit. Put in the work of purposeful exegesis and passionate expository preaching until no one else is left to wonder, "If God didn't mean what He said, then why didn't He say what He meant?"

2

Correcting a Crisis

Our nation is in the throes of turmoil. We are coming off the heels of a global plague (COVID-19). That plague sparked civil unrest as state capitols were desecrated, open riots in the streets were tolerated, and racial tensions were escalated. What's worse, we are witnessing the erosion of our fundamental principles of liberty. Freedom of speech is being whittled away (biblical truths now are being labeled as "hate speech"), the right to bear arms is being challenged, and the freedom of religion is being restricted (especially during the plague). There is a concerted effort to defund the police, which would create even more chaos and instability. We quickly are becoming a nation in which everyone does what is right in his own eyes (Judg 21:25). We are in a crisis.

The sad reality (which few recognize) is that none of those things are the true crisis facing us. They merely are the symptoms. The true crisis is found in the pulpits: a fundamental degeneration in the preservation, protection, and proclamation of Holy Scripture. Until that crisis is confronted and corrected, our nation will keep groaning under the bondage of her corruptions.

Walt Kaiser sounded the warning decades ago, but few had ears to hear. The twin pillars of Christian preaching—namely, hermeneutics and homiletics—were under attack. Once those pillars were corrupted, pulpits were corrupted. Once pulpits were corrupted, churches began churning out "cultural Christians" whose passions for lesser things (political or otherwise) superseded their passion for Christ. Now, many Christians are more passionate about advancing an earthly kingdom than Christ's Kingdom.

Until the pulpit changes, nothing changes. The corrective measure is simple: pure and faithful expository preaching. Expository preaching is the fountainhead of truth from which all correction springs.

Thousands of articles have been written on the need for expository preaching. Yet, few offer a precise definition. Few trace the problem to its original roots. Few pinpoint where sermons depart from exposition. Few offer a step-by-step method of how to do it. We sound the battle cry of "Expository Preaching," as the cure-all, but we rarely equip anyone on what it is or how to implement it. My intention, beginning with this chapter, is to take you on a journey that will help you accomplish three things: (1) interpret Scripture's proclamations with accuracy; (2) discover the timeless principle in Scripture's proclamations; and, (3) apply the Scripture's proclamations with power today. The Holy Spirit has used these principles throughout history to awaken people, congregations, and even whole societies, and the opportunity stands before us for another awakening today.

What is Christian Proclamation?

Christian proclamation is declaring with authority that which God has spoken. The Greek word, "preach" (κηρύσσω), means "to herald" or "to announce." Christian preachers are the King's heralds. As heralds, our God-given task is single: to declare what God has spoken: nothing more; nothing less. Christian preaching is not what you think or feel. Rather, it is the powerful declaration of what the King has spoken. Let me undergird this assertion with two examples from Scripture, one OT and one NT.

First, the OT people of God had been in captivity for many years. They were ignorant of God's Word. God sent Ezra to them. Nehemiah 8:8 says, "They read from the Book, the Law of God, clearly, and they gave the sense, so that the people understood the reading." They read what God wrote. They gave the sense of what God wrote. They helped the people understand what God wrote. That is the formula for correcting a crisis.

Second, the fundamental NT text on preaching is 2 Timothy 3:16. Verse 16 states, "All Scripture is breathed out by God." The Greek word for "breathed out by God" is θεόπνευστος. It is made up of two words: *Theo* (God) + *pneustos* (breathed-out). This speaks of the divine origin of Holy Scripture. Because Scripture comes from the very breath of God, Paul charges Timothy—and us—to preach the Word. Therefore, every genuine preacher must interpret and apply Holy Scripture in such a way that preserves, protects, and proclaims the biblical author's original intent.

Crisis in Hermeneutics

Rarely do we hear God's single meaning extracted, exalted, and expounded. Rather, we hear man's opinions, man's agendas, and man's speculations mingled with God's sacred text(s). This crisis in hermeneutics has profound implications. Think of hermeneutics as the *"science"* of determining what the text meant at the time it was written. I use the word *"science"* in this sense: A set rules for interpretation which are testable and repeatable.

At the heart of the issue is the difference between these two questions:

(1) "What did the text *mean* in its historical context?"

(2) "What does the text *mean* to me?"

These are two different questions entirely, and you must keep them separate. In fact, eliminate the second question altogether. It creates chaos. It produces as many meanings as there are readers, which is precisely why we have the crisis (both in the pulpits and in society). A person can hear ten sermons preached from the same text, and may hear ten different meanings. Why? Because Christian preachers approach Scripture asking, "What does this text mean *to me*?" rather than "What did the author *mean* on the day he wrote it?"

Nehemiah 8:8 is best: (1) read the Scripture; (2) give the author's original intent; and (3) apply it in a way the people understand.

Crisis of Homiletics

I said, "Apply it in a way the people understand," which brings us to the second crisis in Christian proclamation: Homiletics. Think of homiletics as the *"art"* of presenting the biblical author's intent. If flows forth from your hermeneutic.

Corrupt hermeneutics breeds corrupt homiletics.

How do you bridge the gap between what the text *meant* "then," and the significance of that text "now?" Together, we will walk through a step-by-step process to do that. Don't fall into the trap of trying to "make" a text relevant. Scripture is—by its God-breathed nature—relevant. Our task is to: (1) extract the "single meaning"; (2) determine the "timeless principle" imbedded within that single meaning; and (3) apply that timeless principle to present-day mankind.

This is our task. This is the only task that has ever been successful in correcting a crisis.

3

Unmasking Satan's Motive

Do you believe in the sufficiency of Scripture? At times in history, man has held strongly to this conviction. At other times, he hasn't. You can tell when he has or hasn't by looking at the hermeneutics of past eras. Let's take a brief journey to see the ebbs and flows.

Satan's Hermeneutic

Satan craftily disguised his hermeneutic. Consider his first recorded words, "Did God *actually* say . . ." (Gen 3:1). He didn't deny God had spoken. He didn't even try to change the words. Rather, he twisted God's meaning. In effect, Satan asked not, "What do God's words *mean*?," but "What do they mean *to me*?" He shrewdly sought to remove God as the Author of His meaning and replace God with himself. This strategy—offering a deeper (or different) meaning than God intended—was a direct assault on the sufficiency of Scripture. This is where the problem began. Yet, Satan cleverly has repackaged the strategy through the ages.

The Apostles' Hermeneutic (Authorial Intent)

Let's fast-forward to the apostles. Hermeneutically, how did they approach OT texts? Walt Kaiser rightly maintains: "[I]n all passages where the New Testament writers quote the Old Testament to establish a fact or doctrine and use the Old Testament passage argumentatively, they have understood the passage in its natural and straightforward sense."[1] What he's saying is this: When the NT writers engaged in serious exegesis, they handled the text in ways that preserved the OT author's intent. This was the problem Jesus, in large part, was correcting in His Sermon on the Mount. The Pharisees had created deeper (or different) meanings for OT texts in their efforts to control people. Jesus was restoring the biblical author's intent to its rightful place of authority and sufficiency. The apostles, in like fashion, preserved the OT author's intent, and then powerfully applied it to contemporary situations. The result was a proliferation of biblical, gospel truth that changed the world.

---

[1] Kaiser, *Toward an Exegetical Theology*, 57.

The Patristics' Hermeneutic (Allegory)

After the apostles died, two schools of interpretation arose: the Alexandrian and Antiochene schools. The Alexandrian school was famous for its hermeneutic called "allegory." Allegory seeks a deeper (or different) meaning than the author's intent. Their famous teacher, Origen, taught every Scripture text was pregnant with multiple layers of meanings. To him, every text has three meanings: (1) a literal meaning; (2) an ethical (moral) meaning, and a spiritual (heavenly) meaning.[2] We applaud Origen for his high view of Holy Scripture, but we cannot follow him when he says:

> For I think that every extraordinary letter written in the words of God works, and there it not an iota or one dot written in Scripture which does not work its own work in those who know to use the power of the Scriptures.[3]

The Antiochene school, by contrast, insisted allegory was illegitimate and held to the literal meaning alone.

---

[2] See chapter 1 for Origen's fanatical conclusions on the Good Samaritan passage.

[3] Origen, *Homily on Jeremiah*, Fragments from the *Philocalia*, 2.1, trans. John Clark Smith under the title, *Origen: Homilies on Jeremiah; Homily on 1 Kings 28*, The Fathers of the Church, vol. 97 (Washington, D.C.: The Catholic University of America Press, 1998), 278. Origen was commenting on Jeremiah 51:22 in this quote.

They sought to discover the single meaning of the biblical author. They vigorously challenged the Alexandrians, but the impact of the Alexandrians won the day. For centuries thereafter, most Christian preaching drifted into unrestrained allegories. With no interpretive controls in place to hold it accountable, a plethora of heresies sprang forth: works-based salvation, purgatory, indulgences, and many other false teachings.

The Reformers' Hermeneutic (A Return to Authorial Intent)

That dark environment gave birth to the brilliant light of the Protestant Reformation. The motto of the Protestant Reformation became, "*Post tenebras lux,*" which means, "Out of darkness, light." That motto even was printed on the coins in Geneva where Calvin ministered. The Reformers recognized all heresies were connected, directly, to hermeneutical practices. For instance, William Tyndale (ca. 1494–1536) was the first to translate the Greek NT into English. Listen to the hermeneutical philosophy he personally experienced in Roman Catholic universities:

> [T]hey have ordained that no man shall look in the Scripture until he be noselled [nursed] in heathen learning eight or nine years and armed with false

principles with which he is clean shut out of the understanding of Scripture" (*Practice of Prelates*).[4]

The Reformers marched lockstep in rejecting allegory and embracing the principle of *Sola Scriptura*, which means, "Scripture Alone." At its heart, *Sola Scriptura* was a return to the biblical author's single intent. Martin Luther, in many ways the face and personality of the Protestant Reformation, was critical of Origen's method. As mentioned in chapter 1, Luther observed: when the literal meaning is abandoned, "Scripture perishes."[5] He also commented, "[A]llegory is a sort of beautiful harlot, who proves herself specially seductive to idle men."[6] John Calvin went further, deeming allegory "a contrivance of Satan."[7] During the reformation, Luther's common sense approach took root: "The Holy Ghost is the all-simplest writer that is in heaven or earth; therefore his words can have no more than one simplest sense, which we call the scriptural or literal meaning."[8] The effect was a complete reformation of theology, ecclesiology, scholasticism, architecture, culture, etc.: a total reshaping of society. God gloriously blessed that golden era in which the sufficiency

---

[4] See William Tyndale, *Practice of Prelates* (accessible online).
[5] Martin Luther, *Answer to the Hyperchristian*, ... vol. 39 (Philadelphia: Fortress, 1970), 178.
[6] Kaiser, *Toward an Exegetical Theology*, 61.
[7] Kaiser, *Toward an Exegetical Theology*, 61.
[8] Kaiser, *Toward an Exegetical Theology*, 61.

of Scripture was restored to its rightful place of preeminence.

The Post-modern Hermeneutic (Multiple Meanings)

Sadly, that glorious era was short-lived. Over time, Scripture interpretation degenerated into a worse condition than ever. The Reformation gave way to the Enlightenment era (seventeenth and eighteenth centuries), in which all supernatural events in Scripture were either explained away by science or rejected as mere fantasy. The Enlightenment era shifted into the Modernist movement with Charles Darwin, Sigmund Freud, and others: an era in which scientific and psychological ideas were given the first place of preeminence, and those ideas were integrated into Scripture texts.

Modernism gave way to Postmodernism, with its numerous tentacles. Postmodernism no longer limits the text to one meaning (as the Protestant Reformers did) or even three (as Origen did). Nor does it limit the place of preeminence to science or psychology. Postmodernism claims the meanings (plural) in a text are limitless, and the reader takes first place of preeminence. How did they get to that idea?

The German influence of higher criticism taught the author's original intent is impossible to ascertain. Therefore, it is useless to ask, "What did the author mean?" Rather, we should ask, "What do these words mean *to me*, the reader?" That transfer of authority had devastating effects. No longer does a text mean what the author wills it to mean. It means whatever "*I*" want it to mean. That motive was deliberate: to free man from any authority to God (as Author) and to replace Him with every man. Even in 1967, E. D. Hirsch, Jr. lamented: "When critics [readers] deliberately banished the original author, they themselves usurped his place, and this led unerringly to some of our present-day theoretical confusions."[9] Hirsch recognized where all of this was trending: Every man doing that which is right in his own eyes.

The tentacles of Postmodernism kept sprouting. Recently, the idea took a clever turn toward unbridled mysticism. Even in conservative circles, it is common to hear comments like, "God told me . . .," "the Holy Spirit spoke to me . . .," "the still small voice whispered to me . . .," etc. Reminiscent of "inner light" Quakerism, the difference now is the Postmodern mindset has stamped each person's experience with divine authority to his/her own version of truth. This led Oprah Winfrey and others to speak in

---

[9] E. D. Hirsch, Jr., *Validity in Interpretation* (Yale University Press: 1967), 5.

terms of "*your* truth" rather than "*the* truth." That single seed, once sown, has reaped a whirlwind.

More recently, critical race theory and intersectionality (CRT/I) has been embraced by Postmoderns as a legitimate hermeneutical tool. CRT suggests a worldview in which mankind is divided into two groups: "oppressors" and "the oppressed." For instance, CRT claims the social structures in the USA inherently are racist: the laws, judicial system, zoning, tax code, universities, churches, etc. The system becomes a self-perpetuating racist scheme to keep one race in power. This philosophy surreptitiously (or, perhaps deliberately) seeped into Christian hermeneutics.

Hermeneutically, CRT/I proponents approach each Scripture text seeking those two groups: (1) "oppressors" and (2) "the oppressed." The reader, not the author, determines who is in which group, and anyone who disagrees with the reader reveals he is, in fact, part of the "oppressors." In other words, to hold to the biblical author's intent, alone, as absolute truth is the ultimate act of racism. Why? CRT-ers place ultimate authority in their personal (often horrific) experience, not the absolute truth imbedded in Holy Scripture. Anyone who disagrees with them is part of the problem.

CRT/I proponents begin from their personal experience, not absolute truth, and logically trace things backward. They reason, "I have experienced racism because

Unmasking Satan's Motive

the social structures of the USA are inherently racist. Therefore, the Constitution, which gave rise to the country's social structures, must be racist because its framers were all of the same race. Further, those framers largely were informed and influenced by Judeo-Christian ethics found in Scripture. What's more, those Judeo-Christian ethics emanated from the biblical authors' single intent." Therefore, to suggest the authorial intent of the biblical writers is absolute truth is to perpetuate racism. It proves you are part of the "oppressors." The fact that you cannot recognize this means you haven't been "woke." . . . and it keeps on going. This all might seem far-fetched until we look at what is happening in the society around us. Then we start to see realize where the real crisis truly lies: in the pulpits.

I hope this little journey offers perspective. While Satan's tactics change, his motive never does: i.e., to cast doubt on the sufficiency of Scripture. He might mask it through allegory (the Patristics), intellectualism (the Enlightenment), secularism (the Modernists), or the all-out onslaught of multiple meanings (Postmodernism)—now mixed with racially charged innuendos and accusations (CRT/I). It won't stop there. New, repackaged methodologies will emerge in the future, but they are all designed by Satan to put a mask on his true motive: to assault, challenge, dilute, demean, and ultimately deny the sufficiency of Scripture. Remember this: The two glorious eras that unmasked his motive were the two that, hermeneutically, exalted the sufficiency of Scripture. We can do it again in present times: *post tenebras lux*—Out of darkness, light!

4

Why Didn't You Preach What *I* Wrote?

I once saw a long-time preaching professor sitting alone in the cafeteria. I struck up a conversation with him: "What did you preach last Sunday?" He preached from the prophet, Haggai. I asked him the subject of the sermon. I don't remember what he told me, but I remember being stunned. It had nothing to do with Haggai's message. I couldn't help but ask him a simple question, "When you get to heaven and see Haggai, what if he asks, 'Why didn't you preach what *I* wrote?'" The kind-hearted professor honestly replied, "I've never thought about that before."

Expository preaching contemplates that question. It is designed to convey the biblical author's intent. I promised in an earlier chapter ("Correcting a Crisis") to offer a simple step-by-step method for expository preaching. It begins with proper definitions of two terms: hermeneutics and exegesis.

Definition of Hermeneutics

Walt Kaiser defines hermeneutics as the discipline that deals with the principles of interpretation.[1] I described it earlier as a "science" because it is governed by interpretive rules within a system. At its core, hermeneutics is the process concerned with testing the validity of one interpretation over another. The foundation of biblical hermeneutics is grounded upon several pillars of truth:

- Scripture is breathed-out by God and, therefore, inerrant (2 Tim 3:16).
- Scripture is capable of being understood. Modern theologians call this the clarity of Scripture (the Reformers called it the perspicuity of Scripture). Peter mentions that Scripture, at times, can be hard to understand, which the ignorant and unstable twist to their own destruction (2 Pet 3:16). Yet, when we don't understand a Scripture passage, the problem is not with Scripture. The problem is with us.
- God chose to reveal Himself to us through His biblical authors' original intent (2 Pet 2:21).

---

[1] Walter C. Kaiser and Moises Silva, *An Introduction to Biblical Hermeneutics* (Zondervan, 1994), 15.

Therefore, to find the human author's original intent is to find God's intent.
- God's consequences are severe for those who add to or take away from the original meaning (Rev 22:18-19).
- God has not revealed everything to us (Deut.29:29). Some things are not for us to know. Our task is to proclaim what God has revealed, not what He hasn't. Indeed, Paul warns us "not to go beyond what is written" (1 Cor 4:6).

With these foundational principles set, Kaiser drills down a little deeper: "[W]hile hermeneutics will seek to describe the general and special principles and rules which are useful in approaching the Biblical text, exegesis will seek to identify the single truth-intention" of the biblical author.[2] This brings us to the second term we must define: "exegesis."

Definition of Exegesis

Kaiser describes exegesis as the practice of identifying the single truth-intention of the biblical authors in the individual phrases, clauses, and sentences as they make up the thought paragraphs, sections, and ultimately,

---

[2] Kaiser, *Toward an Exegetical Theology*, 47.

entire books.³ If hermeneutics is the *general* discipline that deals with interpretation, then exegesis is the *specific* set of procedures by which we come to the correct interpretation. Exegesis means "to lead out of." It seeks to draw-out the author's single meaning from a biblical text. It is the opposite of "eisegesis." Eisegesis imposes onto a text a different meaning. Typically, this occurs by infusing our pre-understandings, life experiences, or unconscious prejudices into a Scripture text. We always should guard against that. Scripture alone must shape (and interpret) our life experiences, not vice-versa.

Perhaps a contemporary illustration of "eisegesis" will cast light on the crisis in "exegesis." In a recent article in *The Christian Post* (also, *The New York Daily*), theologian Keri Day (professor, Princeton Theological Seminary)⁴ argued white Christians should pay reparations to African-Americans.⁵ She appealed to Zacchaeus's conversion experience in Luke 19:8: "And Zacchaeus stood and said to the Lord, 'Behold, Lord, the half of my goods I give to the

---

³ Kaiser, *Toward an Exegetical Theology*, 47.

⁴ Dr. Day's official title is Associate Professor of Constructive Theology and African-American Religion.

⁵ See Leonardo Blair, "Theologian Makes Biblical Case for Why White Christians Need to Support Reparations for Black Americans," in *The Christian Post* (May 17, 2019), accessible online here: https://www.christianpost.com/news/theologian-makes-biblical-case-for-why-white-christians-need-to-support-reparations-for-black-americans.html. *The New York Daily News* article requires an online subscription, but it was an opinion piece written by Keri Day, entitled, "The Christian Case for Reparations," dated May 10, 2019.

poor. And if I have defrauded anyone of anything, I restore it fourfold.'" Day asserts, "Jesus is clear that reparations or restitution to those who have been exploited and rendered vulnerable is not optional but required."[6]

That statement alone is problematic, but Day goes further: "In his encounter with Zacchaeus, I want to suggest that Jesus sets forth a reparations ethic. . . . Zacchaeus is expected to give back that which he has stolen *so that* he *can be reconciled with others and God*. Reconciliation cannot occur until he has given back what he has stolen."[7]

We appreciate Day for making an honest attempt to interpret the text on its own terms, but she infuses her own situation-in-life into that text. In doing so, she makes two unorthodox claims: (1) that, from Luke's text, Jesus mandated a theology of reparations on all believers and (2) that reparations are *necessary* to attain salvation (i.e., "*so that* he *can be reconciled with . . . God*"). Was Luke's intent in Luke 19:8 to mandate a theology of reparations and a merit-based salvation plan? No.

I'm certain Day is a capable theologian. She simply comes to the Scripture from a different framework. Part of the problem is she incorrectly interpreted Jesus's intent (otherwise she, herself, would be required to make

---

[6] See Blair (quoting Day), "Theologian Makes Biblical Case for Why White Christians Need to Support Reparations for Black Americans."

[7] Blair (quoting Day), "Theologian Makes a Biblical Case . . .," (emphases added).

reparations and restitution to every person she has ever offended). However, the deeper problem is she never attempted to convey *Luke's* intent for including this episode. That point is critical since God chose to communicate this text through Luke.

This is a vivid illustration of eisegesis—imposing a personal experience, passion, or agenda into a Scripture text. This particular example not only changed Luke's intent, it changed the essence of the gospel. I wish I could say this brand of exegesis is an outlier, but it's not. It is the norm.

A Question to Ask

One day we will see the biblical authors in heaven. There will be no condemnation there, of course, but suppose they did ask, "Why didn't you preach what *I* wrote?" It might do well for each of us to ask ourselves that question each time we mount the pulpit. That simple question will drive us to proper hermeneutics and proper exegesis. Perhaps it just might keep us from blushing when we meet Scripture writers—like Haggai or Luke—in heaven.

Context

5

Context, Context, Context

I live in a wonderful little, fast-growing community just outside of Birmingham, Alabama. Real estate is booming. Even small houses are selling for enormous rates. A little house in the middle of town recently listed for a huge asking price. I asked a real estate agent, "How can such a small house command such a large price tag?" His response, "Location, location, location." In hermeneutics, we have a similar saying, "Context, context, context." Context matters.

I'd like to begin to get into the nuts-and-bolts of a term we're learning: hermeneutics. It begins with a proper study of context. We want to understand how the preaching-text fits within the immediate paragraph, the larger section, the book itself, and Scripture as a whole. In our study, we want to move from broader (the message of the whole Bible) to narrower (the meaning of the specific passage under consideration). That begins with a canonical analysis.

Canonical Analysis

What is canonical analysis? Well, the *canon* means the entire Bible. When God gave us the Bible, He gave it to us in chunks spread-out over time—66 separate books written over a time-span of about 1500 years, but it is one story. When God wrote His Book, He had a single purpose in mind. Our first task is to determine that specific purpose. Once we find it, then we must see how our passage fits within that controlling purpose. Canonical analysis, then, is simple: determine the controlling purpose of the Bible.

Our first task is this: *Read the entire Bible chronologically*. If you haven't done this, no worries. Start today, though. Here's a hint that will help you: These 66 books are not in chronological order. They are, more or less, arranged by topic: the Law, the Prophets, the Wisdom literature, etc.

The controlling purpose (we sometimes call it the *canonical center*) of the Bible must come to us "exegetically." I discussed that term in a previous chapter. Simply put, it must spring forth (the "ex" in exegesis) from the text rather than be imposed "into" the text (the "eis" in eisegesis).

Once *everything* is taken into consideration, the controlling purpose that springs forth from Scripture is as follows (from Walt Kaiser):

Context, Context, Context

The plan of God can be defined as a word or declaration from God that he would form a nation and out of that nation he would bring the one through whom salvation would come to all the nations."[1]

Of course, we know that that "One" is the Lord Jesus Christ. Jesus came out of Israel (the tribe of Judah). He brought salvation to people of every nation. The Bible is the stunning story of how God fulfilled that single promise. The OT calls it the "covenant" God gave to Abraham (Gen 12:1-3). The NT—especially Paul—calls it the "promise." Once this *promise-plan* was given, the rest of the Bible is the spectacular unfolding of how God fulfills it in His Son, Jesus Christ. Every paragraph of Scripture, then, feeds into and in some way serves to advance this controlling theme.

David Versus Goliath

Perhaps an example will clarify. Everyone knows the story of David and Goliath. When we understand the controlling theme of the Bible, as stated above, then the meaning of the David vs. Goliath episode becomes much clearer. The focus is *not*: Because David defeated the giant in his life, you can defeat the "giants" in your life, too.

---

[1] Walter C. Kaiser, Jr., *Preaching and Teaching from the Old Testament* (Grand Rapids: Baker Books, 2003), 32.

Rather, the *promise-plan* was in serious jeopardy. The giant, Goliath, defined the terms of battle in 1 Samuel 17:8: "Choose a man for yourselves, and let him come down to me. If he is able to fight with me and kill me, then we will be your servants. But if I prevail against him and kill him, then you shall be our servants and serve us."

Do you see it? The issue at stake was God's *promise-plan*! If Goliath wins, the *promise-plan* perishes. If David wins, the *promise-plan* is preserved. David recognized this clearly. His last words before bull-rushing the Philistine: "The battle is the LORD's, and He will give you into our hand" (1 Sam 17:47). David's trust in that promise was greater than his fear of the giant. You see? This is not about defeating the "giants" in your life so much as it is about trusting God's faithfulness to fulfill His *promise-plan* "in spite" of the giants in your life. That puts this episode in its proper canonical context.

Context Matters

I was teaching this in Senegal, Africa. The following day, a humble African man named Abraham approached me. He was distressed. In his beautiful broken accent, he shared, "I planned to preach David vs. Goliath on Sunday. No one ever taught me about the *promise-plan* of God. I didn't sleep last night. I re-wrote my sermon. May I preach it in class and get your critique?"

This thrilled my soul, but his last words were, perhaps, the most powerful: "Professor, I almost preached in the Name of God something God did not say."

How many times have we done so? Too many, I'm afraid. Not to worry, though. That's what this book is designed to do: Help us refine and sharpen our accuracy in preaching. Where do we begin? Context, context, context.

6

Book Context

Josh Buice once tweeted, "You would never read your grandfather's Last Will and Testament the way many preachers preach the text of Scripture."[1] In a previous chapter, I discussed the significance of "canonical analysis" (determining the controlling message of the whole of Scripture). Let's narrow the focus now to "book analysis."

A book analysis seeks to determine the controlling purpose of the book in which your preaching-text is found. Before you examine your preaching-text, you must ask: Who is writing? Who is his audience? What circumstance prompted him to write? How did he organize (structure) his writing? Finally, what is his single purpose in writing?

A Good Example

For instance, let's say we are studying a passage on the resurrection in the Gospel of John. First, we must

---

[1] Josh Buice, Twitter post, February 4, 2021. https://twitter.com/JoshBuice.

determine John's single purpose for writing his book. Once we know that, the reason he includes so many post-resurrection appearances becomes clear. Thankfully, John is kind enough to state his controlling purpose explicitly. John 20:30:

> Now Jesus did many other signs in the presence of the disciples, which are not written in this book; but these are written so that you may believe that Jesus is the Christ, the Son of God, and that by believing you may have life in His Name.

John's controlling purpose for including so many post-resurrection appearances is to build a case such that there is no compelling reason to deny it, and every compelling reason to believe it. John organizes his book around seven around seven "signs" that Jesus is the Messiah. The resurrection is the final and ultimate "sign." His controlling purpose in all of these "signs" is to persuade the reader to believe that Jesus is the Christ.

Not every biblical author states it so plainly, but if we read a biblical book enough times, the book's overarching purpose will become clear. The meaning of your preaching-text, then, must come under the authority of the author's controlling theme. If it doesn't, then discard it.

Book Context

A Bad Example

A monster movement currently is raging called the New Apostolic Reformation Movement (NAR). In short, they believe the office of apostle disappeared after the first apostles died, and that the Lord has restored it in present times. Ultimately, these modern apostles will lead Christians to take over the world for Christ, largely by infiltrating the existing political structures. NPR did a podcast with one of NARs founders, Peter Wagner, in which he laid-out the movement's premise.[2] We might consider this a fringe movement until we recognize one of their apostles, Paula White, was named a spiritual advisor to a U. S. President. Indeed, I was teaching in Africa, and my African interpreter pulled me aside: "What you are teaching is at odds with what we have been taught." I said, "What have you been taught?" He said, "God granted Christians the dominion to take over the world." I realized NAR had beaten me to Africa.

NAR is corrupting churches primarily by shifting the emphasis of the church *from* justification by faith alone (grace) *to* Christian world dominion (works). They don't necessarily deny justification by faith, which is why it

---

[2] See Terry Gross, "A Leading Figure in the New Apostolic Reformation," on *Fresh Air* podcast on National Public Radio, (10/3/2011); accessible online here: https://www.npr.org/2011/10/03/140946482/apostolic-leader-weighs-religions-role-in-politics.

sounds so "Christian." They merely downgrade it from its central place of preeminence. Ephesians 4:11 is the foundational verse upon which all its other philosophies rest: "And He gave the apostles, the prophet, the evangelists, the shepherds and teachers, to equip the saints for the work of the ministry, for the building up of the body of Christ."

The NAR movement might seem appealing until we ask, "What is Paul's controlling purpose in Ephesians?" Consider the Ephesian context. The congregations were an eclectic mix with a lot of competing interests: (1) Jews/Gentile tensions; (2) converted Gentiles bringing their cultic influences into the church; and (3) imperial worship ("bowing the knee" to Caesar) competing with total allegiance to Christ.[3] Paul doesn't state his controlling theme outright, but you can see how he addresses each of those complexities by how he frames the doctrinal portion of his letter.

- Ephesians 1: We all are predestined *the same way.*

- Ephesians 2:1–3: We all are sinners by nature *the same way.*

---

[3] Frank Thielman does a nice job explaining these complexities. See Frank Thielman, *Ephesians*, Baker Exegetical Commentary on the New Testament (Grand Rapids: Baker Books, 2010), 19-28.

- Ephesians 2:4–10: We all are saved (by grace) *the same way.*

- Ephesians 2:11–22: We all are co-equal citizens in God's spiritual Kingdom in *the same way.*

- Ephesians 3: This spiritual unity remains a mystery to the world, but has been revealed to the church.

Paul's purpose, then, is to bring unity and order to congregations threatened by division from external forces. He did so by addressing the church, not the culture. Ephesians 4:11 was designed, not to bring world unity and world order, but to bring unity and order to Christ's congregations. We can debate whether the office of apostle or prophet exists today, but we cannot use Ephesians 4:11 to justify a world takeover. Why? Because that notion does not come under subjection to Paul's controlling purpose in the letter. Worse, it contradicts it by removing justification by faith as the central priority for the Christian and replacing it with a false gospel rooted in dominion-works. NAR appeals to the fleshly notions of power and status, which is why it is so alluring to many. A simple book analysis would have spared many from the travesties of the NAR movement.

7

Sectional Context and "If My People . . ." Theology

If I were stuck on an island and could have only two books, I'd take the Bible and Walt Kaiser's, *Toward an Exegetical Theology*. It is the most complete book on expository preaching. In it, he discusses the importance of "sectional" context. I have written about *canonical context* ("What is the controlling theme of the entire Bible?") and *book context* ("What is the controlling theme of the book we are studying?"). Now, we must narrow our focus to the specific "section" in which our passage falls.

Sectional context is concerned with determining why the author arranged the material of the book the way he did.[1] Think back to the book context. There, we were seeking a unifying theme of the whole book in a sentence. That unifying them will arise from the text only when we inspect the individual sections.

Kaiser likens it to an auto mechanic. If you disassemble a car, and put all the parts back together again, then

---
[1] Kaiser, *Toward an Exegetical Theology*, 75.

you know how the car works inside and out. The same is true for the expositor. If you disassemble a book, and put it back together again, then you will know it inside and out.

Identifying Markers

Kaiser mentions several clues helpful in marking-off sections of a book.

1. A repeated term, phrase, clause, or sentence. Example: Genesis often repeats, "the generations of . . ." (Gen 5:1, 6:9, 10:1, 11:27).
2. Rhetorical questions. For example: What shall we say then? (Rom 6:1); What then? (Rom 6:15); What then shall we say? (Rom 7:7)
3. A (vocative) shift of attention from one group to another: i.e., Micah 1:2 addresses people in general; Micah 3:1 addresses rulers of Israel; Micah 6:1 addresses mountains of the earth.
4. Transitional conjunctions: then, therefore, but, etc.
5. A change in time, location, or setting.
6. A change in tense or mood of the verb.
7. Some biblical writers make it obvious: i.e., "Now concerning spiritual gifts . . ." (1 Cor 12:1)

Sectional Context and "If My People . . ." Theology

A Good Example

We found the controlling theme of John's Gospel:

> Now Jesus did many other signs in the presence of the disciples, which are not written in this book; but these are written so that you may believe that Jesus is the Christ, the Son of God, and that by believing you may have life in His Name. (Jn 20:30)

That word, "signs," is the clue to how John structured his Gospel. He documented seven signs designed to show Jesus is the promised Messiah. Remember, this must be placed under the "canonical context:" namely, *God promised to form a nation for Himself from Abraham and from that nation bring the One Who would bring salvation to all nations.* John's aim was to prove Jesus is that promised One. What is the proof? These seven signs, the seventh one being the clincher: Jesus rose from death. Let's document those signs quickly.

1. *Changing the water to wine* (Jn 2:11).
2. *Healing the official's son* (Jn 4:54).
3. *Healing the invalid* (Jn 5:16).
4. *Feeding the 5,000* (Jn 6:14).
5. *Walking on water* (Jn 6:16-21).
6. *Healing the blind man* (Jn 9:16).
7. *Raising Lazarus from the dead* (Jn 11:47).

Of course, John then spends chapters 12–21 developing that final, glorious sign: Jesus's resurrection.

A Poor Example

I happened to be at the beach on vacation during the Fourth of July. I attended a worship service, and guess what the preaching-text was? Second Chronicles 7:14:

> If My people who are called by My Name humble themselves, and pray and seek My face and turn from their wicked ways, then I will hear from heaven and will forgive their sin and heal their land.

Predictably, on Independence Day, the pastor proceeded to wag his finger at the politicians and the media and Hollywood and prostitutes and homosexuals and pro-choice advocates, commanding them to repent so God would restore our nation to glory. I don't mean to demean him or his congregation. They were wonderful Christian people. I simply must stop and ask, "Is this the aim of the writer of Chronicles?"

First and Second Chronicles (originally composed as one book) was written after Israel's return from seventy years of exile. John MacArthur opines, "First and Second Chronicles . . . recreate an OT history in miniature, with particular emphasis on the Davidic Covenant and temple worship."² What's more, 2 Chronicles 7 falls within a larger section on Solomon's glorious reign (chs. 1-9) before documenting Israel's infamous fall under succeeding kings (chs. 10-36). In chapter 7 specifically, Solomon just dedicated the temple when Yahweh appeared to him by night, saying, "If my people..."

Clearly, Yahweh was referring to His chosen people, not the American people; to his saints, not to pagans; to His church, not to Hollywood; to believers, not to the intellectual elites in politics, media, and entertainment.

When a pastor is urging pagans to repent while God is urging the church to repent, something has gone wrong.

Nothing the pastor said was untrue. He merely placed his finger upon the wrong text. He proclaimed in the Name of God the exact opposite of what God said *from that text*.

This is precisely the type of preaching which breeds dangerous movements like the New Apostolic Reformation Movement (NAR). They seize on this emotional type of finger-pointing, never realizing judgment begins with the house of God. A simple study on sectional context will keep us from similar embarrassments.

---

[2] John MacArthur, *The MacArthur Study Bible* (Nashville, TN: Word Publishing, 1977), 563.

8

Immediate Context and "Fallen Away from Grace..."

The 1689 London Baptist Confession states of eternal security: True believers "can neither totally nor finally fall from the state of grace, but shall certainly persevere therein to the end, and be eternally saved" (Ch. 17). Yet, Paul says in Galatians 5:4, "You have fallen away from grace." Can we fall from grace or not?

This dilemma sets the stage for a case study in "immediate context." In previous chapters, I have touched on canonical context, book context, and sectional context. Now, we must narrow the focus even more. What is the "immediate context?"

The immediate context investigates how individual paragraphs relate to the larger section. We are concerned with finding the connection between the paragraph under consideration and the larger section in which it is found. A few connecting clues we can seek:

1. *Historical.* There may be a connection of facts, events, or happenings.
2. *Theological.* A doctrine may be dependent on some historical fact.
3. *Logical.* A paragraph may be a sub-point within a larger argument.
4. *Psychological.* A parenthetical "aside," which Paul often includes.

OT Example

Kaiser points to Exodus 6:14-27, a passage in which things weren't going well for Moses.[1] Pharaoh had increased the work-load of the Israelites. The LORD encouraged Moses, promising him (once again) to deliver the people from Egyptian slavery. Exodus 6:14-27 follows, which appears—at first glance—to be a meaningless genealogy. A closer examination reveals much more (see #1 above, the *historical* clue). The paragraph immediately preceding it (Exodus 6:10-12) and the paragraph immediately following it (Exodus 6:28-30) repeat the same point: "Tell Pharaoh king of Egypt . . . But Moses said, 'I am of uncircumcised lips.'" This repetition is important an important clue. Why? When we examine the genealogy, we find it is incomplete: It mentions only three of Jacob's

---

[1] Kaiser, *Toward an Exegetical Theology*, 83-84.

Immediate Context and "Fallen Away from Grace..."

twelve sons (Reuben, Simeon, and Levi). Moses and his brother, Aaron, both came from Levi, so why mention Reuben and Simeon at all? It must be because Reuben and Simeon were as imperfect as Moses. Reuben slept with his father's concubine. Simeon attacked a village without permission after his sister was raped. Now, the genealogy takes on a new light. God gently is reminding Moses (and us) that Reuben and Simeon had faults just like Moses did. The point is not to look at the man, but to look beyond the man to the God Who uses imperfect men to accomplish His perfect will. Yes, even a flawed Moses and a flawed Aaron can accomplish His will! You won't see that unless you investigate how the immediate context fits into the larger section.

NT Example

Galatians 5:4 is a simpler example. I was teaching in Paris, France when a student suggested a believer can lose his/her salvation. He appealed to Galatians 5:4, "You have fallen away from grace." He had isolated that phrase from its immediate context, which led him into doctrinal error.

We patiently showed him the value of investigating the "immediate context." From the beginning of the Galatians letter, Paul has been declaring salvation is by faith alone. Beginning in Galatians 5:2, he entertains a common objection (see #3 above, the *logical* clue). Namely, if someone says salvation comes by law-keeping ("circumcision," verse 2), then he must keep every point of the OT Law to be saved. Otherwise, "you have fallen away from grace." Paul presented a hypothetical to show how preposterous it is to think a true believer can lose his/her salvation. Far from suggesting you can lose your salvation, Paul is declaring the exact opposite: True believers *cannot* fall away from grace. To suggest they could is theologically and logically flawed.

The context, in this case, clarifies the grammatical construction. Some translations render it "you are fallen" (KJV) or "you have fallen" (NAS, NKJV). The Greek word (ἐξεπέσατε) can mean either "fallen," or "fallen away."[2] Walt Kaiser probably is correct to suggest it is a falling away from the *"gospel system of salvation in Christ;"*[3] meaning, the doctrines of grace (more specifically, the *ordo salutis*). Luther likens it to falling from a ship into the sea. He adds:

> To fall from grace means to lose the atonement, the forgiveness of sins, the righteousness, liberty, and life which Jesus has merited for us by His death and resurrection. To lose the grace of God means to gain the

---

[2] BDAG, 307–08.
[3] Kaiser, Jr., *Toward an Exegetical Theology*, 85, emphasis original.

Immediate Context and "Fallen Away from Grace..."

wrath and judgment of God, death, the bondage of the devil, and everlasting condemnation.[4]

Again, here's the point the student was missing: immediate context. He had lifted a phrase and divorced it from its specific role in the section. His mistake was forgivable. We all make mistakes. But the tragedy of his mistake is he turned the whole letter on its head. He made Paul's words say the exact opposite of what Paul intended; and that doctrinal error leads to a false gospel, which was the very reason Paul wrote Galatians in the first place!

How many other heresies have sprung from neglecting to investigate of the immediate context? Too many, I'm afraid. Many are in hell today because someone forgot to look at the immediate context of God's biblical writers. On the other hand, many are rejoicing in heaven today because someone remembered to do so.

---

[4] Martin Luther, *Commentary on the Epistle to the Galatians*, trans. Theodore Graebner (Grand Rapids: Zondervan, 1949), 169-70.

Syntax

9

The Impact of Syntax

When I worked in the legal field, I discovered quickly that words matter, phrases matter, sentences matter, and paragraphs matter. The way you formulate all of those matters, too. I learned this most profoundly when the inheritance of a multi-million estate hung on the correct placement of a single word in a paragraph. When you write a letter or a message, the way you put it together is important to getting your point across. We choose our words carefully—and rightly so—to avoid misunderstanding. The Bible is no different.

God chose His Words carefully, too. Second Timothy 3:16 states, "All Scripture is breathed-out by God." In the original language, the word "Scripture" is the Greek word γραφή (*graphe*). It means God's writings. It is the *graphe*, the actual words that form the sentences and paragraphs, which are breathed-out by God. That is an important point to remember. *Theology* is not said to be breathed-out by God. *Context* is not said to be breathed-out by God. Only the *graphe*, the actual writings, are declared to be God-breathed. The others are important, to be certain, but it is the text itself which commands our attention the most.

Until now, I have focused on context: canonical context, book context, sectional context, and immediate context. Now, we must begin examining the words which God crystallized onto paper from His holy breath: the text itself.

What is syntax? Walt Kaiser says syntax is, "The way in which words are put together so as to form phrases, clauses, and sentences."[1] We particularly are interested, at this point, to distinguish between "main" points and "supporting" points (or sub-points). We want to emphasize what the *graphe* (Scripture) emphasizes; nothing more, nothing less.

Analogy of Antecedent Scripture

In examining syntax, we must keep in mind the "analogy of antecedent Scripture." I will write on this in more detail in a later chapter, but it's so important I wish to plant the seed here. We all have heard preachers who read a preaching-text and then jump all over the Bible to explain it. Theologians call this "systematic theology," which at times can be helpful. However, if our objective is to determine what *this* author is saying in *this* text, then we

---

[1] Kaiser, *Toward an Exegetical Theology*, 89.

must (initially) limit ourselves to the Scripture *this* author knew at the time he wrote. That's only fair, isn't it? We can't expect Paul, for instance, to know what was written in the book of Revelation when the book of Revelation wasn't written until after Paul was dead. And notice, I said "initially." There will come a time when we look at any subsequent revelation (that is, Scripture written after this author wrote). Initially, though, we limit ourselves only to the Scripture our biblical author knew at the time he wrote. This concept will become important later on in the interpretive process. For now, just keep it in mind.

Literary Type

With these principles in place, part of the syntax analysis will be determining the literary type. Common sense tells us we cannot analyze poetry the same way we analyze a parable or a prophecy or an epistle.

There are 5 basic literary types, although some biblical books have variations of these types within them:

1. *Prose.* This is the most common. It is the plain speech of an author. Most of Paul's letters are written in prose.
2. *Poetry.* We all know what poetry is. It comprises about one-third of the OT.

3. *Narrative.* The author shares events. Biblical books like Samuel, Kings, and Chronicles are written as narratives.
4. *Wisdom.* Wisdom literature addresses basic questions of life. Biblical books like Proverbs, Ecclesiastes, and Song of Solomon are examples wisdom literature.
5. *Apocalyptic.* Apocalyptic literature often addresses future events using symbolic language, heavenly visions, and/or past-tense verbs to describe things that have yet to occur (because the author is describing future events that he saw). The book of Revelation is the classic example of apocalyptic literature.

Chapter Divisions

We must remember the *graphe* is God-breathed. The chapter and verse divisions are not. They were dropped-in later as reference points. Often, though, they can trick our minds into breaking the thought-flow.

Here is a brief example. The most difficult of Paul's letters for me to preach through, syntactically, was 2 Corinthians. It is one his least organized letters, probably because it is one of his most personal. Emotion sometimes interrupts thought-flow. For instance, Paul is detailing the changes in his travel plans when, in 2 Corinthians 2:17, he

The Impact of Syntax

off-handedly mentions the "peddlers of God's Word" (i.e., false teachers). The very thought of such "peddlers" triggered a righteous indignation—so much so that he launched into a four-chapter tirade defending his ministry against theirs. I had to read through the entire letter many times before I realized that tirade, really, is a long parenthetical thought that stretches from 2 Corinthians 2:17 through 7:4. In 2 Corinthians 7:4, he picks up again with his travel log. That discovery was not earth-shattering, but it did help me make much better sense of the letter. Most notably, it clued me in to the personal emotion from which Paul wrote. Of all Paul's letters, only Galatians rivals 2 Corinthians in emotive force.

Perhaps that is the salient point to remember regarding syntax. Syntax doesn't always settle-in on the first reading. I read Romans 46 times in a row (not in one day!) before I ever looked at a commentary. Why? I wanted the syntax ingrained into my consciousness before I looked elsewhere. Once I read the commentaries, it became obvious to me which ones had taken the time to let the syntax settle-in. Most jumped right in and started parsing individual words without ever considering how they are connected to the thought-flow of the entire letter.

Take the necessary time to read an entire book—over and over again—before you preach it. You won't regret it. You'll begin to feel the impact of syntax.

10

Does God Care About Paragraph Syntax?

My 11-year old son told me his friends got bored last weekend. They decided to disassemble every part of a microwave. Parts were scattered all over their driveway. Then, they re-assembled it. It was a painstaking process, but now they know that microwave inside and out.

A syntactical analysis does something similar with a paragraph Scripture. It disassembles the paragraph to understand how all the parts work. Then it re-assembles the paragraph so we find what we are searching after: the author's single meaning.

Paragraph Analysis

The majority of your studies should take, as a minimum, one paragraph (sometimes called a "pericope"). Why? Generally, a paragraph expresses a single thought-unit. A paragraph typically consists of two elements: (1) a main proposition and (2) supporting propositions.

Analyzing how any *supporting points* feed into the *main point* is the most tedious (but most rewarding) task we face in interpretation. Why? Because we want to be careful to emphasize what God emphasizes. It will not do to extract a supporting idea and make it dominate the main idea of the paragraph. That runs the risk of changing the author's emphasis, which could change his meaning. Paragraphs typically include 3 parts:

1. *Phrases:* a group of words without a subject and a predicate. An example is, "In the beginning . . ."
2. *Clauses:* a group of words with a subject and a verb. Some can stand alone (independent). Others may not (dependent). An example is John 3:16, "For God so loved the world . . ."
3. *Sentences:* the idea expressed when the two (clauses and phrases) come together to form a complete thought.

Here are five helpful guidelines to follow when studying a paragraph's syntax:

1. *Isolate* the main proposition (the central idea).
2. *Identify* the supporting propositions (the sub-points).
3. *Analyze* the proper weight (emphasis) given to each sub-point.

4. *Search* for any natural divisions in the paragraph (connecting words/phrases, particles, conjunctions, etc.).
5. *Put it back together* and begin to write-out your findings.

You don't need to be overly-technical at this point. You merely are looking for the (1) the main point and (2) the sub-points. It may seem difficult at first, but it is like learning to ride a bike. Once you learn how, you never forget it.

Put it to Practice

A famous example is Ephesian 5:15-23:

[15] Look carefully then how you walk, not as unwise but as wise, [16] making the best use of the time, because the days are evil. [17] Therefore do not be foolish, but understand what the will of the Lord is. [18] And do not get drunk with wine, for that is debauchery, but be filled with the Spirit, [19] addressing one another in psalms and hymns and spiritual songs, singing and making melody to the Lord with your heart, [20] giving thanks always and for everything to God the Father in the Name of our Lord Jesus Christ, [21] submitting to one another out of reverence.

How many times have we heard preachers extract and explode verse 18, "Do not get drunk with wine, for that is debauchery," and then rail against the abuses of drunkenness? While we agree the sin of drunkenness is destructive, we must ask, "Is that the point of this God-breathed paragraph?" Once we disassemble it, examine its parts, and re-assemble it, we find the Apostle Paul had a different emphasis entirely. Let's do it.

1. *Isolate* the main proposition (central idea).

    Paul explained how to live wisely (v. 15a). "Look...how you walk" is an imperative command that governs the rest of the paragraph.

2. *Identify* the supporting propositions (sub-points).

    Supporting Idea #1: Make the most of your time ... (v. 15b-16). This tells how to live wisely. It is subordinate to the imperative, "Look...how you walk."

    Supporting Idea #2: Understand the will of the Lord (v. 17). The word, "therefore," is a clue this is a second idea supporting the command to "Look ...how you walk."

    Supporting Idea #3: Continue to be filled with the Holy Spirit (v. 18-21). The conjunction, "and," tips us off that this a third idea that supports, "Look . . . how you walk."

How do we keep being filled with the Holy Spirit?

> Sub-supporting Idea #1: By spiritual conversation (v. 19a).
>
> Sub-supporting Idea #2: By spiritual songs (v. 19b).
>
> Sub-supporting Idea #3: By continual thanksgiving (v. 20).
>
> Sub-supporting Idea #4: By submitting to one another (v. 21).

3. *Analyze* the proper weight (emphasis) given to each in the passage. We did this in our comments above.

4. *Search* for all natural divisions in the paragraph (connecting words/phrases, particles, conjunctions, etc.). I noted the conjunctions, "therefore" (v. 17) and "and" (v. 18) above. Also, I noticed four consecutive participles: "addressing," "singing," "giving," "submitting." Those participles, which come on the heels of the imperative, "be filled" (πληροῦσθε), flow from that imperative.

5. *Put it back together* and begin to see the author's pattern. From this paragraph breakdown, we have an outline from our study:

Main Point: How to Live Wisely

    I.   Make The Most of Your Time (v. 16)
    II. Understand The Will of The Lord (v. 17)
    III. Continue To Be Filled with The Holy Spirit (v. 18–21)
        A. By Spiritual Conversation (v. 19a)
        B. By Spiritual Songs (v. 19b)
        C. By Continual Thanksgiving (v. 20)
        D. By Submitting To One Another (v. 21)

Of course, no one can do any of these things this apart from gospel-changed heart. Paul addressed that already in chapters 1-3 (sectional context). You would do well to remind your audience as much to avoid preaching straight moralism.

"This is overkill," you say, "It's too technical." Is it, though? I don't think it is. God guided the Apostle Paul to examine OT scriptures syntactically. At one point, the Apostle performs a syntactical analysis, showing how to interpret the word, "offspring"—even noting it is singular, not plural (see Gal 3:15-16). If OT syntax was that important to God, shouldn't it be important to us?

Does God Care About Paragraph Syntax?

That's not to say it isn't tedious work. It is. Yet, it is critically important because often the author's single *meaning* is found in the syntactical construction. Here's how important it is: At least in the case of the Galatian Jews, their syntactical laziness blinded them from seeing their Messiah as the "Offspring" mentioned in their own OT scriptures.

Does God care about syntax? I believe He does.

11

Syntax in Psalm 1

Very few people write about syntax in preaching because it is a technical topic, but we should. Syntax is where the action is when we are searching for God's meaning. I performed a syntactical analysis on an epistle (letter) in a previous article. Now, I'd like to show how to do so on a different *genre*: A psalm. Common sense should tell us: We cannot approach an epistle the same we approach poetry.

Gospel Reminder

Lest we be accused of preaching "morality," we must frame our preaching within the context of the gospel. I typically do this by pointing to how God saves sinners. Paul's classic *Ordo Salutis* ("Order of Salvation") describes the process:

1. Election
   (God's sovereign choice of a people for Himself)

2. The Gospel Call
   (Holy Spirit summons sinners to God)
3. Regeneration
   (Holy Spirit resurrects the dead soul to life)
4. Conversion
   (sinner repents & turns to Christ by faith)
5. Justification
   (God legally declares the sinner as righteous)
6. Adoption
   (God formally accepts redeemed sinners into His family)
7. Sanctification
   (Holy Spirit conforms them into Christ's image)
8. Perseverance
   (believers persist in obedience until death)
9. Death
   (the redeemed sinner's mortal body expires)
10. Glorification
    (the saint receives an immortal body).

Every text falls within one of these categories. Most psalms fit, generally, in the "Sanctification" category. Although, certain elements of the other categories will be mixed in as well.

Disassemble Psalm 1

Let's perform a syntactical analysis in alignment with the process set forth in chapter 10.[1] Psalm 1 reads:

> ¹ Blessed is the man who walks not in the counsel of the wicked, nor stands in the way of sinners, nor sits in the seat of scoffers; 2 but his delight is in the law of the LORD, on His law he meditates day and night. ³ He is like a tree planted by streams of water that yields its fruit in its season, and its leaf does not wither. In all that he does, he prospers.
>
> ⁴ The wicked are not so, but are like chaff that the wind drives away.
>
> ⁵ Therefore the wicked will not stand in the judgment, nor sinners in the congregation of the righteous; ⁶ for the LORD knows the way of the righteous, but the way of the wicked will perish.

1. *Isolate* the theme proposition or sentence (also called central idea).

---

[1] Kaiser, *Toward an Exegetical Theology*, 171. Kaiser diagrams this passage in Hebrew and shows the constructions in a helpful way. My chapter sticks with the English, recognizing most haven't studied Hebrew.

Theme proposition: Righteous people will have quality character and (productivity).

2. *Identify* the supporting propositions (also called sub-points).

Supporting idea #1: God Approves Some (1:1-3).

Blessed is the man . . .

Sub-supporting idea "A:" He has consistent conduct (1:1b).

> who walks not in the counsel of the wicked, nor stands in the way of sinners, nor sits in the seat of scoffers;

Sub-supporting idea "B:" He has constant delight (1:2).

> but his delight is in the law of the LORD, on His law he meditates day and night.

Sub-supporting idea "C:" He has quality character (1:3).

> He is like a tree planted by streams of water that yields its fruit in its season, and its leaf does not wither. In all that he does, he prospers.

Syntax in Psalm 1

Supporting idea #2: God Disapproves Others (1:4-6).

> The wicked are not so . . .

Sub-supporting idea "A:" His weak character (1:4b)

>> but are like chaff that the wind drives away.

Sub-supporting idea "B:" His end (1:5).

>> Therefore the wicked will not stand in the judgment, nor sinners in the congregation of the righteous;

>>> Sub-sub-supporting idea "1:" The knowledge of the Lord (1:6a).

>>> Sub-sub-supporting idea "2:" The judgment of the Lord (1:6b).

3. *Analyze* the proper weight given to each in the passage.

4. *Search out* all natural divisions in the paragraph (studying punctuation, particles, conjunctions, etc.).

    1:1 not, nor, nor

1:2 but
1:3 natural division: example of righteous.
1:4 natural division: clear break (wicked).
1:5 therefore (signals conclusion)
1:6 for (signals purpose)
1:6 but (signals contrast)

5. *Reassemble* the text.

Central Theme: Godly Character Leads To Godly Productivity

    I. God Approves Some (1:1-3).
        A. Consistent Conduct (1:1b).
        B. Constant Delight (1:2).
        C. Quality Character (1:3).
    II. God Disapproves Others (1:4-6).
        A. Weak (Poor) Character (1:4).
        B. Judgment Day (1:5).
            1. The Lord's Knowledge (1:6a).
            2. The Lord's Judgment (1:6b).

Someone once suggested to me, "You could preach the same sermon in a Jewish synagogue as you could in a Christian congregation, and no one would know the difference." This is where the *"Ordo Salutis"* comes to our rescue. Our concern above was to analyze God's breathed-out syntactical constructions. I will discuss (in detail) in a later chapter how to deliver the message in a Christocentric context without violating the biblical author's single meaning.

12

Does Jesus Care About Syntax?

Does Jesus care about syntax? We often read His parables as their own, isolated units. Yet often more is going on outside the parable than inside it. Take the case of the prodigal son (Luke 15:11–31). You must filter through three different authorial intents to determine the single meaning:

1. the parable's intent;
2. Jesus's intent in telling it; and,
3. Luke's intent for including it.

The first two are important, but the third—Luke's intent—is governs the other two.

The Prodigal Son

The prodigal son is one of the most beautiful passages in Scripture. It's almost always told in the context of evangelism: A heartwarming story of heart-felt repentance, glorious renewal, and jubilant restoration. It's about a wayward son who realizes the unconditional love of the father. It's about music and dancing and happy times—but is it truly about happy times?

A closer look reveals a sad ending, not a happy one. We *do* see repentance, renewal, and restoration of the younger brother. Yet when we ask ourselves (1) "What is Jesus's purpose in the story?" and (2) "What was Luke's purpose for including it?" we discover Jesus's purpose is not to highlight the happy times. Quite the opposite—His purpose was to uncover the jealousy of the older brother. You see, everyone in the whole chapter is happy and excited except for one person: the older brother. He's angry, jealous, critical, and unforgiving. To see it, we must study the syntax.

The Prodigal Son Context

Luke 15:1-2 provides the context. Jesus was talking to sinners and tax collectors. Some Pharisees were present, too. The Pharisees begin grumbling about Jesus eating with such sinners. Jesus responds with three parables, but it's really one big story.

He tells of a sheep that was lost and then found. *There was great rejoicing.* He tells of a coin that was lost and then found. *There was great rejoicing.* He tells of a son who was lost and then found. *There was great rejoicing*—but then the pattern breaks. Jesus closes with the reaction bitter, older brother, Luke 15:25–32:

> Now his older son was in the field, and as he came and drew near to the house, he heard music and dancing. And he called one of the servants and asked what these things meant. And he said to him, "Your brother has come, and your father has killed the fattened calf, because he has received him back safe and sound." But he was angry and refused to go in.
>
> His father came out and entreated him, but he answered his father, "Look, these many years I have served you, and I never disobeyed your command, yet you never gave me a young goat, that I might celebrate with my friends. But when this son of yours came, who has devoured your property with prostitutes, you killed the fattened calf for him!"
>
> And he said to him, "Son, you are always with me, and all that is mine is yours. It was fitting to celebrate and be glad, for this your brother was dead, and is alive; he was lost, and is found."

Do you see what Jesus is saying? This whole three-parable set is in response Pharisees' critical comment to Jesus, "This man receives sinners and eats with them" (15:2). Jesus is turning the tables on the Pharisees: "You, Pharisees, are acting like the older brother!" It is this "break" in the parable-pattern that sets it off as the central purpose. Everyone in the parables is rejoicing except the older brother. Everyone around Jesus was celebrating except the Pharisees. You can see it in the syntax.

The Prodigal Son Syntax

Jesus is telling the Pharisees: *You* are the older brother. *You* are the "angry" ones (15:28). *You* are resentful—he refused to go in (15:28). *You* claim you have served your father these many years (15:29). *You* claim you never disobeyed the commands (15:29). *You* did this ritual and followed these rules and those regulations, but your heart is calloused. *You* have critical spirits, resentful spirits, prideful spirits.

Indeed, the personal pronouns of the older brother confirm this: "*I* have served you" (15:29); "*I* never disobeyed" (15:29); "You never gave *me* a young goat" (15:29).

Again, Jesus is answering the question, "Why do I eat with the sinners and tax collectors?" The answer comes in the third parable: Because "it is fitting to celebrate and be glad, for," the sinner and tax collector. Why? Because they, like the younger brother, were spiritually dead and now are alive; they were lost, and now they have been found. *You*, Pharisees, are acting like the older brother—grumbling and criticizing as sinners are receiving God's grace.

Does Jesus Care About Syntax?

If there were any doubts, Jesus hits the bullseye in Luke 16:14:

> The Pharisees, who were lovers of money, heard all these things, and they ridiculed Him. And He said to them, "You are those who justify yourselves before men, but God knows your hearts. For what is exalted among men is an abomination to God."

The Parable's Relevance

The root problem was diagnosed by the father: an unforgiving heart. "I forgave your brother," he pleads, "Why can't you?" And so it was with the Pharisees: God was saying, "I have forgiven these sinners and tax collectors. Why can't you?"

1. Purpose of Parable: Uncover the unforgiving heart of the brother.

2. Purpose of Jesus: Uncover the unforgiving heart of the Pharisees.

3. Purpose of Luke: Luke states the purpose of his book in 1:4: *To provide certainty to Theophilus concerning the things he has been taught.*

Indeed, this parable-set provides certainty by showing why the Pharisees, like the older brother, were seeking to silence Jesus: their hearts were hard. In fact, Jesus revealed their motive in His next breath, a parable exposing their greed (Luke 16:14).

Syntax matters. It mattered to Jesus. It should matter to us, too.

13

Word Meaning Matters

At the supper table one night, my mother said, "Eat your potato chip." I love potato chips, but I didn't see any. I looked at my sister's plate. I looked at both my brothers' plates. I looked under the table. "Eat your potato chip!" she said again, more forcefully. I bumped my head on the way up, it startled me so! For the life of me, I couldn't find any potato chips. My mother, now irritated, exclaimed for the third time, "I said, 'Eat your potato chip!'" Utterly confused, I finally replied, "I don't see any potato chips."

She looked at me strangely, then smiled, then started laughing, which sent the entire table (except for me) into deep belly laughs. Finally, after catching her breath, my mother explained. "I didn't mean, *Eat your potato chip.* I meant, *Eat your potato, Chip!*"

Then I looked at my plate: A piping hot baked potato sat right in front of me the whole time!

Verbal meaning matters.

Verbal Plenary Inspiration

Verbal plenary inspiration means "every word found in the Bible is given to us by God (verbal), everything in the Bible is authoritative (plenary), and every word is divinely directed."[1] I believe we all would agree: God carefully chose every single word in Scripture. Words are the building blocks of meaning. My "eat your potato chip" example is enough to illustrate a word can have several different meanings.

Consider the word, "world." Scripture uses it in different ways:

1. Planet earth — Romans 1:20
2. Materialism — Mark 8:36
3. Secular system — Romans 12:2
4. Lost souls — John 14:17
5. Limited geographical region — Romans 1:8
6. Unlimited geographical region — Matthew 24:14

---

[1] Matt Slick, "What is Verbal Plenary Inspiration of the Bible?" *Christian Apologetics & Research* (Oct 27, 2014). If you haven't read B. B. Warfield's magisterial work, *The Inspiration and Authority of the Bible* (1948), you must. It has yet to be adequately refuted.

7. Secular mindset   Matthew 13:22

8. Earthly realm   John 12:25

Verbal Plenary Principles

Is there a process we can apply to determine which usage is the correct one? Certainly. Follow the guidelines below. Make sure you follow them in order.

1. Determine the meaning of the word at the time the author wrote. For instance, today we use the word "hope" to refer to a wish: i.e., I "hope" it doesn't rain tomorrow. When Paul wrote, the word didn't mean "wishful thinking." It meant a rock-ribbed assurance: a future certainty not yet realized. That's why he says in Romans 12:12: "Rejoice in hope." You rejoice in certainty, not in a possibility (wish).

2. Investigate how the same author used the word in other places:

   a. First, investigate how he used the word in the rest of the book under consideration.

   b. Second, investigate how he used the word in his other writings.

3. Research how other biblical writers used the term.

4. Run a search on how extra-biblical writers of the same era uses the term.

Once you've cycled through these steps, see if that meaning aligns with the surrounding context.

Verbal Plenary Example

I recently came across this one while preaching through Romans. In Romans 7, Paul described the conflicted Christian—that emotional tug-of-war between the spirit and the flesh within every believer.[2] Paul even cries out in despair, "Wretched man that I am!" (Rom 7:24). It's as if he says, "I want to do right, but I don't always do right! How can this be? Am I even saved? . . ."

The chapter break after verse 25 is unfortunate because the thought-flow carries into Romans 8:1: "There is therefore now no condemnation for those who are in Christ Jesus" (Rom 8:1). Intuitively, I thought that word, "condemnation," referred to "self-condemnation." That is, self-induced guilt. Yet, it never made much sense to me because I *do* experience self-induced guilt when I sin, but this verse says "no condemnation." So I did a word study.

---

[2] I understand some (see Schreiner in BECNT) think Paul is describing the unconverted Jew, but this is a minority view. While a possible view, the context of Romans 5-6 suggests Romans 7 is dealing with the Christian's battle with the mortification of the flesh.

First, what did "condemnation" (κατάκριμα) mean when Paul wrote it? *BDAG* says it is, "a judicial pronouncement upon a guilty person."[3] Paul is saying, "There is therefore now no death-sentence. The death penalty has been removed!"

That changed my understanding. When I fail in my fight against sin, the death-penalty is not hanging over my head. It has been removed. That glorious news reinvigorates me to go back to battle with a renewed spirit. I can fight without the pressure of thinking, "If I fail, the death penalty awaits."

Second, does Paul use this term anywhere else in this letter? Yes, he does in two other places. Romans 5:16: "And the free gift is not like the one man's sin. For the judgment following one trespass brought condemnation." Ah, there is confirmation I'm on the right track! The Apostle uses it again in Romans 5:18: "Therefore, as one trespass led to condemnation for all men . . ." Ah! A second confirmation. Now, I feel reasonably comfortable I'm onto Paul's meaning.

Third, if I wanted to be thorough, I could search it in Paul's other letters (it doesn't occur in any of them in that Greek form).

Fourth, if I wanted to be more thorough, I could search it in the entire NT (again, that Greek form doesn't occur).

---

[3] *BDAG*, 518. *BDAG* notes the word not only denotes the pronouncement of guilt, but also the adjudication of it.

Fifth, if I wanted to be extra thorough, I could search it in the LXX (the Greek translation of the OT: it doesn't occur there either).

Finally, if I wanted to turn over every rock, I could search it in secular Greek literature. *BDAG* did this and came the definition above. It was a judicial term.

You see, I was imposing my twenty-first century understanding on a first-century word! Words can take on new meanings over time. Do the necessary work to make certain you are understanding God's words the way the biblical author meant them to be understood. If only I'd known this principle when I was seven years old: I'd have saved myself a bump on the head while looking for those potato chips!

Interpretation

14

Head Coverings and Cultural Norms

Our interpreter greeted us in Nigeria by holding my hand. I felt a little uneasy about that. I attempted to pull back my hand, but he wouldn't let it go. He kept holding my hand as if he hadn't a care in the world. A few more paces, and I could take no more. I pulled my hand from his and said, "Where I come from, we don't do that." He got a good laugh at my expense before explaining that, in Nigeria, it is normal for close friends to hold hands. What I thought was an offensive gesture between two males was, in reality, a gesture of goodwill in his country. This was my introduction to Nigeria and to "cultural norms."

Cultural Norm Principles

Cultural norms can change over time. They also might be different in different places. For example, contracts in OT Bethlehem were executed by removing your sandal and giving it to the other party (Ruth 4:7). Such a cultural norms were unique to a specific times and places. We must be aware of that as we seek to determine the author's intent. Here are some guidelines to consider:

1. Identify those items unique to the specific times, culture, and situation of the biblical author.

For instance, the congregations in Rome faced a certain cultural development in the first century. While Jews were a minority in the city of Rome, they likely were a majority in the congregations (Rome seems to have had several house congregations; see Rom 16). However, in AD 49, Emperor Claudius expelled all Jews from Rome. The congregations quickly became majority Gentile. Whereas before, the congregations were majority Jewish, now the Jew/Gentile relationship was much more complex. There seems to be real tension there. Paul addresses each group specifically at times (see Rom 11:13).

If you are unaware of that cultural setting, as well as the Jewish cultural norms regarding diet, rituals, and calendar days, then it will affect how you understand certain passages in Romans. Romans, more than any other letter, explains precisely how God saves sinners—but for a purpose: the obedience that springs from saving faith (1:5; 16:26). Regarding the ethnic tensions, specifically, Paul desired to bring both ethnicities to a place of harmony, united as a single spiritual race in Christ Jesus. Only the gospel can do that through changing hearts by faith. Paul masterfully explains how in Romans, but you have to know that specific time, culture, and situation to grasp the letter's brilliance.

2. Determine what is *prescriptive* from that which is *descriptive*.

The first NT congregations were communal. Acts 4:34-35 states, "There was not a needy person among them, for as many as were owners of lands or houses sold them and brought the proceeds of what was sold and laid it at the apostles' feet, and it was distributed as any had need."

This is *descriptive*, not *prescriptive*, because other NT congregations—such as Corinth (2 Cor 9:7), Ephesus (Eph 4:28), and Thessalonica (2 Thess 3:10) were not communal.

Other teachings, such as limiting the office of pastor to males, clearly, are *prescriptive* (1 Tim 3:1-7; Tit 1:5-9; cf 1 Cor 14:33-34; 1 Tim 2:11-15) because they were written to multiple congregations in multiple geographic locations, but the message is consistent in each locale.

3. Distinguish a *cultural norm* from a *biblical principle*.

Greeting someone with a "holy kiss" (1 Cor 16:20) in the first century was a *cultural norm*. Today—in North American culture—"shaking hands" (not holding hands!) is the *cultural norm*.

4. Recognize when God offers a reason for a cultural norm to extend to all believers of all ages.

First Corinthians 11:3 declares, "The head of every man is Christ, the head of every woman is her husband, and the head of Christ is God." Because this principle is rooted in the nature of the Godhead, then the husband is to always be head of the wife in all Christian marriages across all cultures.

Cultural Norm Example

We don't have space for a detailed exegesis, but let's explore 1 Corinthians 11:4-6 briefly. Paul mentions this strange custom of women wearing head coverings when they pray. No one can agree whether these were hoods, bonnets, handkerchiefs, veils, or even long hair.[1] However, they all agree it was some type of covering of the head. When I researched the cultural norms in Corinth, I discovered the following:[2]

---

[1] See David E. Garland, *1 Corinthians*, Baker Exegetical Commentary on the New Testament (Grand Rapids: Baker Academic, 2003), 517.

[2] Some feel that head coverings are *prescriptive*, since God grounds it in the Trinity (1 Cor 11:3) and in creation (1 Cor 11:7-9, 12). However, the submission of a woman to her husband (or father, if not married) is the *prescriptive* principle grounded in the Trinity and in creation (not the external symbol of a head covering).

Head Coverings and Cultural Norms

1. In Corinth, head coverings were worn by women in public as a sign of submission, sexual purity, and devotion to their husbands (or, if not married, to their father).[3] They functioned much like a wedding ring in North American culture.

First, neither Paul nor any other NT writer mention this head covering custom to any other NT congregation. The NT writers do emphasize the woman's submissive role repeatedly (Eph 5:22; Col 3:18; 1 Tim 28-14; Tit 2:3-5; 1 Pet 3:1-6, etc.).

Second, literature from the first century, and even statues in Corinth, confirm Corinth's cultural norms: (1) men wore short hair; (2) women wore longer hair; and, (3) the first century writer, Tacitus, states a husband would cut (or shave) the hair of his adulterous wife for shame. See Garland, *1 Corinthians*, 517-30.

Third, Bruce Winter presents compelling evidence of a first century women's empowerment movement in the Roman empire in which women were pushing back against traditional roles. See Bruce W. Winter, *Roman Wives, Roman: The Appearance of New Women and the Pauline Communities* (Grand Rapids: W. B. Eerdmans Publishing, 2003).

Taken together, God is most concerned that (1) Christian women were/are submissive in their heart and (2) that such submission was/is expressed through reasonable cultural norms where God has placed them. For instance, wives in India wear red powder on their foreheads; Tibetan wives wear aprons; North Americans wear rings, etc. Christian converts who cast off these symbols of submission in Christian worship are making a rebellious statement (to God, the congregation, and the culture), which is what was happening in Corinth. The letter is quite clear: the women (as well as the men) were filled with pride and dominance rather than humility and servitude.

[3] Garland, *1 Corinthians*,), 514, states, "The veil indicated the woman's marital status." John MacArthur, *1 Corinthians*, The MacArthur New Testament Commentary (Chicago, IL: Moody Press, 1984), 255, states, "It seems, therefore, that Paul is not stating a divine universal requirement but simply acknowledging a local custom. The local Christian custom, however, reflected the divine principle."

2. A woman who uncovered her head was considered promiscuous or risqué.[4]

3. A woman whose hair had been shaven was a public sign of shaming, which indicated she had committed adultery. It functioned much like the adulteress's scarlet letter "A" in Nathaniel Hawthorne's, *The Scarlett Letter*.[5]

4. Pagan worship in Corinth included *men* actually covering their heads. It was seen as a symbol of submission to the pagan god being worshiped. For instance, a statue existed in Corinth of the Roman emperor, Augustus, offering a liquid sacrifice with his toga pulled over his head.[6]

When we consider these cultural norms, the passage makes more sense:

- 1 Cor 11:4 - Men were adopting the pagan worship custom of covering their head with their toga (as

---

[4] Garland, *1 Corinthians*, 520-21, states, "Uncovering the head in public had sexual implications . . . Women who went uncovered in public gave nonverbal clues that they were 'available.'"

[5] Garland, *1 Corinthians*., 520, "The shaved head is imposed upon the adulteress to expose her publicly." MacArthur, *1 Corinthians*, 257, states, "Chrysostom records that women guilty of adultery had their hair shaved off and were marked as prostitutes."

[6] See Garland, *1 Corinthians*, 517, who presents credible and verifiable historical evidence of the practice of head covering in pagan worship throughout the Roman empire.

Head Coverings and Cultural Norms

the statue of Augustus depicted).[7] Paul informs them not to do that. It would bring dishonor to Christ. Further, women in Corinth's culture wore head coverings as a sign of submission to their husband (or father). For a man to cover his head would confuse God's ordained roles. It could be construed as a sign of upsetting God's created order; an order God established and grounded in the nature of the Godhead (1 Cor 11:3) and in creation (1 Cor 11:7-9, 12).

- *1 Cor 11:5* - Here again, a woman in Corinth's culture wore a head covering as a symbol of respect and authority toward her husband (or father, if not married). A woman who cast off the head covering would reflect a cavalier and prideful attitude. Worse, it would be seen as rebelling against God's created order.

- *1 Cor 11:6* - If a woman is so cavalier as to flaunt herself as promiscuous and risqué, then she may as well shave her head like the adulterer because that is how she is acting anyway.

---

[7] Garland, *1 Corinthians*, 517, points to, "The statue from Corinth of a veiled Augustus—with his toga pulled over his head. . . . Because of the clear association of this practice with pagan devotion, pulling the toga over the physical head in Christian worship would shame the spiritual head of the man, Christ."

This is why John MacArthur concludes, "The apostle is not laying down an absolute law for women to wear veils or coverings in all churches for all time, but is declaring that the symbols of the divinely-established male and female roles are to be genuinely honored in every culture."[8]

Cultural Norm's Relevance

I once had an African interpreter in Senegal, a powerful orator named Stephen. He was never taught this principle of cultural norms. He returned the next morning and said, "The principle of cultural norms saved my congregation!"

His African congregation was on the verge of splitting over the issue of head coverings. He called them together the night after our class. He explained the principle of cultural norms to them. It cleared up the matter entirely. Everyone went home happy and in harmony. The Holy Spirit enlightened them to the timeless principle imbedded in

---

[8] MacArthur, *The John MacArthur Study Bible*, 1745. See also, Garland, *1 Corinthians*, 522, "Although Fee (1987:512) is correct that Paul's instructions are tied to cultural norms that are relative and that literal obedience is not required to be obedient to God's word, . . . Paul's concern that Christians honor sexual decorum in worship and avoid what a culture deems to be suggestive attire is a broadly applicable, through elastic, concept." Garland was referring to Gordan D. Fee, *The First Epistle to the Corinthians*, New International Commentary on the New Testament (Grand Rapids: W. B. Eerdmans, 1987), 512.

that text. Namely, God rooted in the creation the roles and responsibilities of husband and wife. The Apostle Paul was more concerned that wives (1) submit to their husbands and (2) respect their God-given gender role from an obedient heart—whatever form that takes in a given culture (head covering, wedding ring, etc.).

All it took was understanding the cultural norms the biblical author was addressing in a first-century Greek congregation to bring a twenty-first century African congregation into perfect harmony.

15

Scripture Interprets Scripture

We often think allegorists have no interpretational controls; that allegory is free association gone wild. Yet, even the prince of allegorists, Origen, actually held (loosely) to two interpretational parameters: (1) the analogy of Scripture (*analogia scriptura*) and (2) the rule of faith (*regula fidei*). Regarding the former, he advocates "'comparing spiritual with spiritual,' and interpreting each passage according to the usage of Scripture writers."[1] Regarding the latter, he plainly states the teaching of the Church "alone is to be accepted as truth which differs in no respect from ecclesiastical and apostolical tradition."[2] Augustine (also loosely) followed suit.[3] Both Luther and Calvin appealed to Romans 12:6 to support the "rule of faith," too. Henry Blocher's older but excellent article

---

[1] Origen, *Contra Celsus* 7.11 (ANF, 4:615).
[2] Origen, *De Principiis* Praef., 2 (ANF, 239).
[3] Augustine's views essentially are the same as Origen's. For his view on the *analogia scriptura*, see Augustine, *On Christian Doctrine* 3.26, 27, 28; for the *regula fidei*, see 3.2, 5.

traces how, for the Reformers, the "rule of faith" became synonymous with "Scripture interprets Scripture."[4] My next chapters will tighten the screws further by setting forth the "analogy of *antecedent* Scripture," but for now, here is the idea: If you encounter a word or phrase you don't understand, sometimes another verse of Scripture might cast light on it.

Analogy of Scripture Process

Try this process (similar to the word study process I wrote about in chapter 13).

1. *Consult clearer verses written in the same book you are studying.* If a verse in Romans is unclear to you, does Paul clarify matters anywhere else in Romans?

2. *Consult other biblical writings by the same author.* If a verse is unclear to you in Romans, does Paul broach the subject with more clarity in another of his letters?

---

[4] See Henri Blocher, "The 'Analogy of Faith' in the Study of Scripture," in *Scottish Bulletin of Evangelical Theology* 5 (1987): 20. As well, the 1689 London Baptist Confession states, "The infallible rule of interpretation of Scripture is the Scripture itself; and therefore when there is a question about the true and full sense of any Scripture (which is not manifold, but one), it must be searched by other places that speak more clearly" (1.9).

3. *Open-up your investigation to parallel passages written by other Scripture writers.* If you are in Matthew's Gospel, does Mark or Luke or John mention the same situation?

Example of the Same Writer Clarifying

Colossians 1:15 states, "He is the image of the invisible God, the firstborn of all creation." The term, "firstborn," created quite a stir for about 55 years between two men in church history: (1) Arius, a priest and (2) Athanasius, a deacon (who later became bishop of Alexandria). Both were located in Alexandria, Egypt in the fourth century. Their conflict was over the nature/deity of Christ, and it all came down to a single word, "firstborn."

Arius believed Jesus was finite. To him, Jesus was the "firstborn" in this sense: He was "created" as the first act in creation. Arius famously opined, "If the Father begat the Son, then He Who was begotten had a beginning."[5] It follows that the Son is subordinate, not co-equal, with God the Father, a view known as subordinationism.

Athanasius believed Christ was an infinite Person in the Godhead. To him, Jesus was the "firstborn" in this sense: He held supremacy in rank. In Bible times, the

---

[5] Socrates Scholasticus, "Ecclesiastical History," *Nicene and Post-Nicene Fathers of the Christian Church*, series 2, vol. 2 (1957), 3.

firstborn son was held in great honor. Athanasias believed Christ is eternal, co-equal with God, and the "firstborn" Who outranks all other created beings.

For fifty-five years, the debate kept going. Finally, in AD 325, the first ecumenical church council was convened, the Nicene Council, to settle the matter. Athanasius won the day, and the doctrine of the Trinity became codified in the Nicene Creed. However, Jehovah Witnesses today still hold Arius's position, which is why they deny the Trinity— and it all came down to one word, "firstborn."

Had they followed our process, we could have saved them fifty-five years and terrible turmoil!

1. *Does Paul use this word anywhere else in Colossians?* Yes, in verse 18. Jesus is "firstborn" from the dead. However, we read of others in the OT and NT who rose from the dead before Jesus did, so Jesus must be "first in rank" (not the first to rise from the dead).

2. *Does Paul use the world anywhere else in his other letters?* Yes. He uses it Romans 8:29: "For those whom he foreknew he also predestined to be conformed to the image of his Son, in order that he might be the firstborn among many brothers." Here, Paul clearly is speaking in spiritual terms. He was not speaking of one "born first" physically. Rather, he

Scripture Interprets Scripture

was declaring Jesus was the "first in rank" among all of God's elect children.

3. *Does any other NT writer use the term?* Yes; Luke, John, and the author of Hebrews used the term. Luke 2:7 does use it in a physical sense: Jesus was Mary's "firstborn" son. The writer to the Hebrews uses it three times: twice as "first in rank" (Heb 1:6, 12:23) and once as physical "firstborn" (Heb 11:28—referring to the death of the "firstborn" at Passover. Finally, John uses it in Revelation 1:5 as "first in rank"—Jesus was "firstborn" from the dead. Again, Jesus wasn't the first to rise from the dead. We think of Eutychus, Jairus's daughter, Lazarus, and others. However, He was the "first in rank" to rise and never die again.

Having completed this simple exegetical process, we must make some conclusions. First, we must have the intellectual honesty to admit the word *can* mean "firstborn" physically on rare occasions. However, the context makes it explicit when it does. Here, the surrounding context and grammar evidence supports the assertion that Paul meant "first in rank." We agree with Athanasius. The glorious, historic doctrine of the Trinity stands.

Example of Another Biblical Writer Clarifying

Walt Kaiser offers another example.[6] Luke 14:26:

> If anyone comes to Me and does not hate his own father and mother and wife and children and brothers and sisters, yes, and even his own life, he cannot be My disciple.

The word, "hate," is troublesome because it seems to contradict the fifth commandment: Honor your father and your mother . . . (Ex 20:12). A word study reveals it means "to be disinclined to, disfavor, disregard."[7] Do other passages cast light on this dilemma?

1. *Does Luke use it anywhere else in his Gospel?* He uses it six other times, all in terms of the world's hatred for Christ and His followers. These usages don't help us much.

2. *Does Luke use it in his other writing, Acts?* No. We have a dead end here, too.

3. *Do any other NT writers use it?* Yes, it's used 33 times by various NT authors (other than Luke), but none offer much clarity for us. However, one parallel

---

[6] See Kaiser, *Toward an Exegetical Theology*, 126.
[7] *BDAG*, 653.

Scripture Interprets Scripture

passage might help. Matthew 10:37: "Whoever loves father or mother more than Me, is not worthy of Me. And whoever loves son or daughter more than Me is not worthy of Me." Matthew is making the same point to a different (Jewish) audience, but his description his revealing. Now, we begin to understand Luke's intent more precisely: Your love for Jesus must be so overwhelming that your love for father or mother pales in comparison.

Try this little 3-step process as you go. It will keep you tethered to the biblical author's intent . . . as well as keep you from falling into Arian, anti-Trinitarian heresies!

16

Is Christ in Every Text?

In seminary, a fellow student once told me, "We must preach like the apostles preached. They proof-texted freely and found Christ in every text." I looked at him strangely and replied, "But I'm not an apostle. I'm not called to make new revelation. I'm called to preach what the apostles wrote."

Most proof-texting is innocent enough. However, it quickly can become a dangerous game that, without controls, leads to destructive heresies and a different Christ (2 Cor 11:4). Ask Paul. He dealt with unbridled proof-texters nearly everywhere he went: Galatia (Gal 1:8), Corinth (2 Cor 11:13), Colossae (Col 2:16-23), and Ephesus (1 Tim 1:3-7; 2 Tim 2:16-18) to name a few.

Does this mean we are never allowed to proof-text? No, but it does mean we need a carefully thought-out strategy. Before you proof-text, consider the following:

1. "Initially" limit yourself to the "analogy of antecedent Scripture."

2. Preserve the biblical author's original intent in your preaching-text.

3. Introduce any subsequent revelation in summaries and conclusions.

Antecedent Scripture

I wrote in the previous chapter of the "analogy of antecedent Scripture." Briefly, that principle declares: If our single aim is to determine the biblical author's original intent (and it is), we *initially* must limit proof-texts to passages the biblical author knew at the time he wrote.

This is only reasonable. For example, Paul couldn't have known the contents in the book of Revelation when he wrote Romans since Revelation hadn't been written. It would be unfair, then, to superimpose passages from Revelation onto Romans (eisegesis). However, it *is* justifiable to cite passages that informed the biblical author's meaning.

Subsequent Revelation

May we ever cite texts written later? Absolutely. However, the order matters. Follow this order: (1) once our *initial* study is complete, and (2) we have determined our biblical author's original intent, *then* (3) it is (entirely) appropriate to consider any subsequent revelation that may cast light upon our preaching-text. In fact, it would be disingenuous to withhold it. I only caution: It's best to introduce any subsequent revelation in summaries or conclusions so as not to lose the uniqueness of the preaching-text.[1] This upholds the sufficiency of Scripture while preaching the whole counsel of God.

Canonical Center

One other issue must be taken under consideration: What is the controlling theme of the whole of Scripture? I discussed this, too, in a previous chapter, but it all comes to bear at this point in the interpretive process. Walt Kaiser defines the canonical center of Scripture this way:

> [T]he plan of God . . . that he would form a nation and out of that nation he would bring the one through whom salvation would come to all the nations.[2]

The Bible, then, is the stunning story of how God freely gifted that promise to sinful mankind and fulfilled that promise in His Son, Jesus Christ. Every paragraph of Scripture either feeds into or flows out of this canonical

---

[1] Kaiser sounded this warning, too, in, *Toward an Exegetical Theology*, 140.
[2] Walter C. Kaiser, Jr., *Preaching and Teaching from the Old Testament* (Grand Rapids: Baker Academic, 2003), 32

center and—in some way—serves to advance God's glorious redemptive purpose in Christ.

But Isn't Christ in Every Text?

The rage for the last couple of decades or so has been to find Christ in every text. Often, this is done by prooftexting or "word associations" from later texts. This practice was fueled by a slew of preaching books in the late 1990's and early 2000's: books like Graeme Goldsworthy's *Preaching the Whole Bible as Christian Scripture*. The idea is the whole Bible is centered on Christ. The trick to preaching, they suggest, is to find Christ in every text, and draw Him out for all to see. Proponents call this the "Christocentric" approach (as if our approach is not Christocentric).

We agree the whole Bible centers on Christ in that every text "points" to Christ. However, to dig underneath the text for a deeper, Christocentric meaning is allegory. No one likes to hear that, but such a methodology seeks a "deeper" meaning than the biblical author intended. A better approach is to read the Bible forward, not backward. Rather than searching for Christ in every text, our task is to decipher the biblical author's original intent and show how that intent is fulfilled in God's *promise-plan*, which centers on Jesus Christ. Or, as Spurgeon once recounted, "Now, where is the road to Christ?"[3]

David and Goliath

Abraham Kuruvilla's excellent article illustrates the fallacy of the "Christ-in-every-text" approach.[4] He notes Goldsworthy takes David as a type of Christ (the Anointed One) and Goliath as a picture of sin and death. Thus, the David and Goliath episode serves to foreshadow "God's Christ (Anointed One) wins the victory over sin and death on behalf of his people."[5] Peter J. Leithart, a Presbyterian theologian goes further,

> The fact that he is described as wearing "scales" indicates that Goliath was a serpent. Once again there is a serpent in the garden-land of Israel.... David was the new Adam that Israel had been waiting for, the beast-

---

[3] A quote often is attributed to Spurgeon is, "I take my text and make a beeline to the cross." Spurgeon never appears to have made this comment, but he certainly agreed with it in principle. In Spurgeon's 1859 sermon, "Christ is Precious to Believers," he favorably recounts an old Welsh minister telling a young minister, "[F]rom every text of Scripture there is a road to... Christ. And, my dear brother, your business is when you get to a text, to say, 'Now, where is the road to Christ?'"

[4] Abraham Kuruvilla, "David V. Goliath (1 Samuel 17): What is the Author *Doing* with what He is *Saying*?" in The Journal of the Evangelical Theological Society 58/3 (2015): 487–506.

[5] Graeme Goldsworthy, *Gospel and Kingdom* (Exeter: The Paternoster Press, 1981; Minneapolis, MN: Winston Press, 1982), 73.

master taking dominion over bears and lions and now fighting a "serpent."[6]

To this, we merely ask a simple question, "Is this what the biblical author of Samuel meant?" No, the biblical author highlighted how God used David's child-like faith in His *promise-plan* to preserve the nation, Israel, and to bring forth from that nation the One Who would redeem all nations.

The implications of such allegorical tendencies, however, are far-reaching. If no NT author makes those connections (and no NT author does), then we implicitly are grooming hearers to trust human speculation rather than the sufficiency of Holy Scripture.

Abiding Implications

This leads us to our present state of confusion. We have sowed allegorical seeds to the wind, and we are reaping the whirlwind of Postmodernism; and now, the vain philosophies of man which emerge from Postmodern mindsets. For instance, some modern evangelicals no longer reinterpret individual texts through Christ's cross-event. Rather, they reinterpret texts through Christ's mission, which to them, is not so much to save sinners as it is

---

[6] Peter J. Leithart, *A Son to Me: An Exposition of 1 & 2 Samuel* (Canon: 2003), 98, 100.

to protect the oppressed from the oppressors. Every passage in Scripture, then, is interpreted in the light of personal experience ("your truth," they say), not the biblical author's intent (absolute truth), a move Southern Baptists adopted with Resolution 9 in Birmingham in 2019. Resolution 9 offers license to take the biblical narrative of David and Goliath in the same direction as the homosexual rector of Episcopal Church of Holy Communion (Missouri), Mike Angell. In his June 21, 2015 sermon, Angell proclaims,

> Our Goliath isn't a person, it's an ideology, it's a system. Our Goliath was created as women and men from Africa were forced into chattel slavery. My ancestors enhanced the racial biases they inherited. They created and codified a system of race that haunts us today.... It feels like we are on the front lines, still, and still our Goliath wakes up in the morning to taunt us. The Bible tells us that Goliath walked back and forth jeering the Israelites for forty days. Forty days is the Bible's way of saying "a really long time," too long. We have been waiting for the end of racism for too long. Why won't this Goliath leave us alone?[7]

---

[7]Angell was formerly Assistant Rector at St. John's Church, Lafayette Square, Washington, DC. He was awarded the John Hines preaching award, which "celebrates the ministry of preaching and its importance in our Church by recognizing outstanding sermons that are

David, of course, represents anyone who has the courage to stand up against alleged systemic racism. This example might have been but a footnote had not Angell won the internationally recognized John Hines preaching award for this type of allegorical preaching. Of course, that was in 2015. Today, we've moved past that to calling on white congregations to pay reparations to black congregations. As noted in a prior chapter, Princeton theologian, Keri Day, is demanding $500 million from white churches and synagogues. She justified such a demand from Jesus's encounter with Zacchaeus in Luke 19.

How did we get to this place? We didn't think carefully through (1) how to proof-text properly and (2) how properly to weight subsequent revelation in the sermon. Now, Holy Scripture has become a weapon, which each man or woman wields for his or her own agenda(s).

---

deeply grounded in scripture and focused on the seen and unseen needs of the worshipping community, the nation and the world."

17

Is a Text Pregnant with Meanings?

For centuries, theologians have grappled with the tension between the human author(s) and the Divine Author of Scripture. Historically, this has caused the church great turmoil, leading some to see two, three, four, or even more meanings in every text. As we near the end of our interpretive (exegetical) process, we must consider the question, "What is the relationship between the human author and the Divine Author in Scripture?" Space limits a full-orbed historical survey, but the following historical sweep will put the discussion in its proper context.

Historical Sweep

Philo, a Jewish philosopher born in 20 BC, suggested every OT text had two meanings. He felt the Hebrew scriptures were too culture-specific. He attempted to make the OT more palatable to a Greco-Roman culture by broadening the meaning of passages, especially the Levitical laws.

A two-meaning system developed: (1) the literal meaning and (2) a hidden one.[1]

Origen (late second century) suggested every text had three meanings. He was influenced heavily by Platonism and attempted to synthesize three streams of thought: (1) the human author; (2) the Divine Author; and (3) his contemporary Platonic thinkers. He developed a tri-partite structure: (1) the literal (human author's meaning); (2) the heavenly (Divine meaning); and, (3) the ethical (moral meaning).[2] Origen did apply two controlling parameters: Every interpretation must align with (1) the analogy of Scripture and (2) the rule of faith.[3]

Augustine (late fourth/early fifth century) reached further, suggesting every text had up to four (or more) meanings. His words:

> When, again, not some one interpretation, but two or more interpretations are put upon the same words of Scripture, even though the meaning of the writer intended remained undiscovered, there is no danger if it can be shown from other passages of Scripture that

---

[1] For example, see Philo, *De Specialibus Legibus*, 1.37.207-208. In 1.37.207, Philo suggests the hidden meaning underneath the washing of the feet of animals is that man's soul should walk upward to heaven.

[2] See Origen, *De Principiis*, 4.1.11. In support of this three-fold division, Origen cites Proverbs 22:20-21: "And do thou portray them in a threefold manner, in counsel and knowledge, to answer words of truth to them who propose them to thee."

[3] See Origen, *Contra Celsus*, 7.11 and *De Principiis*, Praef., 2.

Is a Text Pregnant with Meanings?

any of the interpretations put on the words is in harmony with Scripture.[4]

Augustine developed a system in which a text might have as many as four meanings: (1) historical (what has been done); (2) aetiologial (why it was done); (3) analogical (consistency between OT & NT); and (4) allegorical (the Divine meaning). Augustine, too, applied two controlling parameters: Any interpretation must align with Jesus's command to "love God and love your neighbor."[5]

Augustine's influence trickled down through the medieval age. Thomas Aquinas formalized it into what became known as the *Quadriga*, which the Catholic church employs with some regularity even today. Aquinas posited four meanings: (1) literal (human author's meaning); (2) tropological (moral); (3) anagogical (future fulfillment of divine promises); and (4) allegorical (the Divine meaning). Over time, the literal meaning began to be usurped by the other three. Extra-scriptural traditions began to take root from the "non-literal" meanings (indulgences, limbo, purgatory, works-salvation, etc.), resulting in a two-source authority: Scripture and tradition. Oberman and Ward, respectively, track this progression in their excellent works.[6] What we find is the Divine Author's

---

[4] Augustine, *On Christian Doctrine* 3.27.
[5] See Augustine, *On Christian Doctrine*, 1.36.
[6] Heiko Oberman, *The Dawn of the Reformation: Essays in Late Medieval and Early Reformation Thought* (Edinburgh: T&T Clark, 1986), 276–

meaning(s)—which was subject to the interpreter—began to overshadow the human author's meaning.

The Protestant Reformers rescued us from such polyvalent meanderings, in large part, by restoring the human author's intent to its rightful place of objectivity. As noted earlier, Martin Luther said of Origen:

> That is why Origen received his due reward a long time ago when his books were prohibited, for he relied too much on this same spiritual meaning, which was unnecessary, and he let the necessary literal meaning go. When this happens Scripture perishes and really good theologians are no longer produced. Only the true and principal meaning which is provided in the letters can produce good theologians.[7]

Their battle cry was *Sola Scriptura* ("Scripture alone"), which was nothing less than a return to the human author's intent. The human author's intent was much more objective. I could be substantiated through his (1) grammar/syntax and (2) historical context. The so-called Divine Author's intent had been abused and weaponized to keep people (as well as the original human author) in

---

280; Timothy Ward, *Word and Supplement: Speech Acts, Biblical Texts, and the Sufficiency of Scripture* (Oxford: University Press, 2002), 21–73.

[7] Martin Luther, *Answer to Hyperchristian, Hyperspiritual, and Hyper-learned Book by Goat Emser in Leipzig—Including Some Thoughts Regarding His Companion, the Fool Murner, 1521*, in *Luther's Works* (Fortress: 1970), 178.

subjection. Only the objective truth of the human author's intent could cut through such subjective, oftentimes fanatical, conjectures. Sadly, the revival of the human author's meaning was short-lived.

Higher criticism, in the nineteenth and twentieth centuries, threw up its hands and suggested no one can know the human author's meaning (Schleiermacher, Gadamer, Frye, Derrida, etc). Therefore, the reader—not the author—determines meaning, which paved the way for where we are today: full-blown Postmodernism.

Though brief, this historical sweep suggests all of these efforts were grappling with the same question: What is the relationship between the human author's meaning and the Divine Author's meaning?

The Problem Continues

After this brief historical journey, one might think we would take all precautions against suggesting every text is pregnant with multiple meanings. Yet, the urge to dabble has proven too fascinating. Mitchell L. Chase's recent article is stimulating, even if highly speculative.[8] He relies

---

[8] Mitchell L. Chase, "A True and Greater Boaz: Typology and Jesus in the Book of Ruth," *The Southern Baptist Journal of Theology*, 21.1 (2017): 85–96. Chase is an adjunct professor at Boyce College.

heavily on David Schrock[9] and, to a lesser extent, Jim Hamilton.[10] We respect all three men as capable theologians and solid exegetes. Yet, we must point out areas where we might disagree slightly.

Chase advocates for a controlled typology. That is, any typological connection must be grounded in (1) historical correspondences, (2) a discernible escalation between type and antitype, and (3) a Christological viewpoint. He supports this assertion with Schrock, who departs slightly further from the human author's intent: "[I]t is appropriate to speak of typology in terms of Christotelic trajectories *that would have exceeded the expectations of the original author and audience . . . Israel's persons, events, and institutions are divinely designed types of Christ.*"[11]

We must pause here to ask, "Who decided on these three criteria? If trajectories exist that exceed the human author's expectations, how do we know it? Who authorized it? Certainly no NT author; and if no NT author, then who?"

We cannot help but notice: The transference of meaning, subtly, has shifted from the human author to the human interpreter; and this sleight of hand (intentional or not) flies under the guise of the Divine Author.

---

[9] Schrock is an adjunct professor at Boyce College and The Southern Baptist Theological Seminary.

[10] Hamilton is a professor at The Southern Baptist Theological Seminary.

[11] Schrock, "What Designates a Valid Type?," 25 (emphasis added).

Is a Text Pregnant with Meanings?

Chase further asserts, "The divine author has designed a type to function in a forward-pointing, christotelic way."[12] To this, we must pause again—with eyebrows raised—and ask, "On what basis do we make such a leap? On inferences grounded purely in human speculation? And, then, are we to preach speculations as if they carry Divine Authority?"

Chase continues, "The NT authors never claimed to exhaust all that one can see of Christ in the OT, nor did they forbid their readers from imitating their hermeneutics."[13] Once more, we must pause to consider the (perhaps unintended) implications of this statement. We understand Chase's point, but what of Paul's instruction to the Corinthians "not to go beyond what is written" (1 Cor 4:6)? Whatever Paul meant by that, it was within the context of the Corinthians elevating their human wisdom above what is written.

Finally, Chase asserts, "While readers can be certain about Christological types which NT authors have identified [with this, we agree], interpreters can also make a cumulative case *suggesting* a type, which is unidentified by NT authors, with different *degrees of probability* or certainty."[14]

---

[12] Chase, "A True and Greater Boaz: . . . ," 87.
[13] Chase, "A True and Greater Boaz: . . . ," 88.
[14] Chase, "A True and Greater Boaz: . . . ," 88 (brackets and emphases added).

Here, we must ask, "Who defines these 'degrees of probability,' and how? What is the objective measuring-stick?" Chase even suggests (quoting George Barrois) that to *not* enter into such speculative typology is a "serious fault of method."[15] Barrios, now deceased, ought to have known where this leads, historically, since he was a professor (and historian) at Princeton Theological Seminary.

Chase will go on to suggest Boaz is a type of Christ, a notion we shall examine in more detail in a subsequent chapter. Before we drink too deeply from this rather stimulating well, though, someone must be willing to ask the most pertinent question of all, "Is this what the biblical author's truth-intention in all of this?"

This is not to suggest Chase, et al., are not capable theologians. They are. Likewise, they are well-intentioned, and we recognize their motive is pure: to glorify Christ in new, exciting dimensions. They make valid points and offer Christ-centered controlling parameters. Moreover, they have centuries of church history on their side.

Yet, that is precisely the point. Origen and Augustine offered reasonable controlling parameters, too (see above). Nevertheless, when they stepped away from the objectivity of the human author's intent, it was a slow, slippery slope into subjectivism. The end-game of subjectivism nearly always leads us to the same terrible place:

---

[15] Chase, "A True and Greater Boaz: ... ," 88.

Is a Text Pregnant with Meanings?

An inherent or outright denial of the sufficiency of Scripture.

This typological proposal is a dangerous one—indeed, one we cannot accept—and the record of church history is the strongest evidence of where this road leads. One can see, easily, how this interpretive laxity opens "Pandora's Box" of pregnant meanings. We don't need better controls on typological references—the Holy Spirit made plain, through the NT apostles, the typological references He desired us to have. Rather, we need a (re)commitment to true and principal meaning of the human author through whom God chose to speak.

The position detailed above is predicated on a massive presumption: namely, that we possess the same hermeneutical powers as the apostles—another proposal we cannot accept. The apostles' hermeneutical powers were stamped with infallibility, inerrancy, and a certainty we do not enjoy. We don't need to apologize for this. If the NT authors make typological (or hermeneutical) correspondences, then we are on solid footing. Otherwise, it is a serious fault of method—and a dangerous one—to create those ourselves and then proclaim them as divinely authoritative.

Is There a Solution?

So far, we have done nothing except uncover the problem which has plagued interpreters, ancient and modern; namely, "What is the relationship between the human biblical author(s) and the Divine Author." Is there a solution? Indeed, there is. It begins with the two principles: (1) the *analogy of antecedent Scripture* and (2) the distinction between the human author's *meaning* and the timeless *significance* of that meaning. To these, we shall turn next.

18

Closing the Gate on Allegory

We detailed earlier how, historically, an issue that has plagued interpreters is the relationship between the human author(s) of Scripture and the Divine Author. What is the relationship between the two?

First, since the Divine Author chose to communicate His will for mankind through human authors, then the human author's meaning (often called the "literal meaning") *is* the Divine Author's meaning. What's more, the Divine Author chose to give us the Bible progressively. Therefore, we must respect the way in which God progressively revealed Himself. This makes the *"analogy of antecedent Scripture"* all the more important to close the gate on the allegorical tendencies we have witnessed throughout history.

Analogy of Antecedent Scripture

The analogy of antecedent Scripture acts as one gatekeeper which protects against multiple meanings rushing-in to corrupt the biblical author's single truth-intention. Kaiser notes:

> The only correction that we know for past and present abuses that have taken place in the name of doing theological exegesis is to carefully restrict the process to (1) examination of explicit affirmations found in the text being exegeted and (2) comparisons with similar (sometimes rudimentary) affirmations found in passages that have *preceded* in time the passage under study.[1]

This means we read the Bible forward, not backward. That is, we must (*initially!*) limit any theological observations (or proof-texts) to scriptures the biblical author knew at the time he wrote. Indeed, we must be deliberate *not* to allow later revelation to alter or influence the biblical author's intent at the time he wrote. Once our exegesis is complete, however, we would be remiss if we failed to trace-out any subsequent theological developments in our summaries or conclusions. Again, this is only reasonable since it respects the way God gave us the Bible:

---

[1] Kaiser, *Toward an Exegetical Theology*, 161 (emphasis original).

progressively. Abuses creep in when we begin interpreting the Bible backwards.

We are so serious about this point that we must sound an alarm: The greatest threat to accurate Christian proclamation is a violation of this principle, and the last fifty years of preaching bear that out. Today, we see pastors/theologians who decry allegory while actively, though oftentimes unwittingly, engaging in it![2] Largely, this is done by imposing later theological grids, developments, or proof-texts of which the biblical author was unaware at the time he wrote. Those who question the analogy of antecedent Scripture do so on the basis of two rather bold assertions: (1) I merely am exposing the Divine Author's meaning and (2) I merely am employing the same hermeneutical principles as did the NT apostles.

To this, Kaiser responds:

> The whole approach is wrongheaded historically, logically, and biblically ... The tendency to interpret the Bible backward is a serious procedural problem, for it will leave a large vacuum in our teachings and provide seedbeds for tomorrow's heresies.[3]

---

[2] My dissertation documented that over half the sermons at the Southern Baptist Convention Pastor's Conference displayed "strong" allegorical tendencies. This was over a decade's span. See Chipley McQueen Thornton, *Allegorical Tendencies and Their Relation to the Doctrine of the Sufficiency of Scripture* (2009).

[3] Walt Kaiser, *Preaching and Teaching from the Old Testament* (Baker: 2003), 26.

Indeed, our previous chapter documented those seedbeds and the terrible heresies which sprang from them (and are still bearing their rotten fruit).

Perhaps you have become frustrated when someone took your words out of context. That experience can be maddening. It stands to reason, then: we should offer the biblical human authors the same courtesy we expect from others. Perhaps a couple of examples will illustrate.

A Good Example

Romans 10:13 is a clear case of "intertextuality:" i.e., one biblical author citing another biblical author who preceded him in time. Paul states: "For 'everyone who calls on the Name of the Lord will be saved.'" He is citing the OT prophet, Joel (2:32). Obviously, the Apostle Paul's had studied Joel's prophecies, and they informed Paul's theology. So let's investigate Joel's assertion.

Joel 2:32 states: "And it shall come to pass that everyone who calls on the Name of the LORD shall be saved [Paul cites this part of the verse]. For in Mount Zion and in Jerusalem there shall be those who escape, as the LORD has said, *and among the survivors shall be those whom the LORD calls*" [Paul did not cite this part of the verse]. Joel 2:32b, which Paul did not cite, tips us off to something important: which is, Joel actually defines who will call upon the Name of the LORD—it is only those whom the LORD effectually calls. Paul didn't bring this part to the attention of his hearers. It was unnecessary. He had treated God's elective purposes already in Romans 9, but Joel's theology certainly informed Paul's. The analogy of antecedent Scripture, then, gives us a valuable piece of direct evidence to that effect. We now are on solid footing, given this direct piece of evidence to assert: Just as the elect in Joel's day would be saved by faith alone, so the elect in Paul's day will be saved by faith alone.

A Not-So-Good Example

Theologians have long-suggested Boaz is a type of Christ, even though no NT author makes that connection. Mitchell L. Chase recently argues as much and builds his case based on seven "correspondences": (1) Boaz was from Judah's tribe—Christ was from Judah's tribe; (2) Boaz was from Bethlehem—Christ was born in Bethlehem; (3) Boaz redeemed Ruth—Christ redeems sinners; (4) Boaz welcomed foreigners—Christ welcomes Gentiles; (5) Boaz was overly kind—Christ is overly kind; (6) Boaz kept the law—Christ kept the law.[4]

All these "coincidences" sound alluring until we ask a simple question, "Is this what the human author of Ruth intended to convey?"

---

[4] Chase, "A True and Greater Boaz: . . . ," 85–96.

In fairness to Chase, he begins with the human author's intent: To show how God providentially arranged the lineage of King David. At this point, however, he begins interpreting the Bible backward, imposing later revelation onto Ruth's author. So alluring and exciting are his analogies that we even start to think, "All these connections can't be merely coincidences, can they?" Chase himself states, "It cannot be coincidental that *go'el* appears twenty-two times in the Book of Ruth, the precise number that the word appears in Leviticus."[5]

Yet, if it were *that* obvious, how did the NT authors miss it?

Have we, in all this excitement, perhaps inadvertently shifted the emphasis from the biblical author's single truth-intention to the reader's probability recognitions? And, amidst this shift of emphasis, some (like us) are left still asking, "Does the biblical author's single truth-intention mean anything at all?" Or, is it merely a springboard to greater and more exciting imaginative speculations?

When we ask such questions, we quickly are met with the famous assertions we refuted in the previous chapter: "One, I have the same hermeneutical powers as the NT authors; and two, I have uncovered the Divine Author's meaning that the NT authors neglected to mention."

---

[5] Chase, "A True and Greater Boaz: . . . , 91.

Could it really be that the NT authors dropped some grain in the corners of the interpretive field for those coming behind them to glean (i. e., Ruth 2:2)? We remain unconvinced.

Close the Gate

The previous example, at the least, opens the gate for allegory to enter in. Yet, we are still left wondering, "Is there a disciplined way to preach Christ from the Book of Ruth which is grounded in biblical authority?" Certainly.

The single truth-intention of Ruth's author is as follows: To show how God providentially arranged the lineage of King David. The five-verse genealogy that closes the book makes that obvious (Ruth 4:18-20). This truth-intention must be preserved and emphasized to the degree the biblical author emphasized it; and, in this case, the whole book is structured to bring us to those verses. Otherwise, we run the risk of doing violence to the original author's intent.

That genealogy connects Boaz as the great-great grandfather of King David. King David is considered Israel's greatest king, the one who united and expanded the kingdom of Israel. Subsequent revelation in the NT—specifically, Matthew 1:1-17—traces traces Jesus Christ's lineage through King David. Further, Peter proclaimed that One greater than King David has been exalted to the right

Hand of God (Acts 2:24–36). This direct NT evidence removes any presumption and assures us we are grounding our proclamation in biblical authority. So, Boaz played a critical and providential role in bringing forth the Messiah, Jesus Christ, into the world. In the Divine Author's progressive revelation, the brightness of this future development deserves and demands to be showcased in the sermon.

This method retains and respects the uniqueness of the human author's intent, reads the Bible forward (not backward), and exalts Christ as the ultimate fulfillment of God's unfolding *promise-plan*. In response, every person is left to conclude the following: If God could use commoners like Boaz and Ruth to exalt a Righteous One to His right Hand to rule and reign eternally . . . then maybe He can use a commoner like me to glorify the Promised One, too.

19

Bridging the Gap Between *Then* and *Now*

A lot of contemporary preaching loses biblical authority in that gap between what it meant "then" and its significance "now." In that gap, preachers often (inadvertently) sever the author's meaning from its contemporary significance. This "bridging the gap" is the subject of John Stott's classic book, *Between Two Worlds*. Stott writes that "preaching is not exposition only but also communication, not just the exegesis of a text but the conveying of a God-given message to living people who need to hear it."[1] If the biblical author controls the meaning (and he does), then he also controls the contemporary significance of his meaning.

Until now, we've focused strictly on the process of hermeneutics: what the text meant "then." Now, we must start thinking in terms of its relevance today. This launches us into a new process called homiletics. Simply

---

[1] John Stott, *Between Two Worlds: The Challenge of Preaching Today* (Grand Rapids: W. B. Eerdmans, 1982), 137.

put, homiletics is the *art* of presenting God's single meaning in a way people will understand. In Nehemiah 8, the children of God returned from captivity, largely ignorant of God's Word. Nehemiah 8:8 says, "They read from the book, from the Law of God, clearly, and they gave the sense, so that the people understood the reading." Homiletics focuses on the *"giving-the-sense-so-that-the-people-understand-it"* part. The first step in homiletics is to determine the timeless principle.

Determining The Timeless Principle

If the biblical author's meaning is fixed (and it is), then the Holy Spirit has placed in every text of Scripture a fixed timeless principle. The timeless principle is that single principle derived from the biblical author's single intention, which applies to all people of all times. How do we determine that timeless principle? Jay Adams's excellent little volume, *Truth Applied*, offers 5 questions to keep us on track.[2]

1. What is the situation?

    a. What is going on?

    b. What is addressed?

---

[2] Jay E. Adams, *Truth Applied: Application in Preaching* (Grand Rapids: Zondervan, 1990), 54.

2. Who is doing what about the situation?

    a. To understand it?

    b. To change it?

    c. To complicate it?

3. How does God view the situation?
4. What response does He require?
5. What is the Spirit's purpose?

Study the progression of these questions. They move us from what God said *then* to how that meaning applies *now*.

An OT Example

Adams points to Paul's example in 1 Corinthians 9:7-11. Paul cites Deuteronomy 25:4 to support his assertion that gospel ministers should be paid for their labors. Deuteronomy 25:4 says, "You shall not muzzle an ox when it is treading out the grain." Adams explains, "Paul saw in the Deuteronomy passage a principle that applied to oxen but also to all sorts of work situations."[3]

The larger context of Deuteronomy 25:4 addresses laws which encourage fairness and generosity. Paul recognized that God "breathed out" these laws to His people

---

[3] Adams, *Truth Applied*, 47.

for a purpose: to promote moral growth in attitudes of fairness and generosity. The "meaning," then, is limited to Moses's intent as it relates to oxen (or attitudes of fairness in general), namely, oxen deserve to be rewarded for their labor. The *timeless principle* names a relationship between that meaning and the present-day audience: that is, if an ox is rewarded for his labors, the gospel minister should be rewarded for his labors, too. The examples given by Moses in Deuteronomy were not meant to be an exhaustive listing or even ends in themselves. They were specific examples of how God-honoring people should behave in general. In other words, the application is not so wooden as to suggest the congregation pay their minister in grain and oats (or tomatoes and cucumbers, as some congregations seem to think!). Obviously, those examples served as illustrations to encourage fairness and generosity not only toward God's beasts, but also toward His gospel ministers.[4] Paul argues his right to be paid is based on the *timeless principle* imbedded in Deuteronomy 25:4. Although he possesses that right, he chose to refrain from exercising it.

---

[4] Kaiser, "The Current Crisis in Exegesis and the Apostolic Use of Deuteronomy 25:4 in 1 Corinthians 9:8–10," *JETS* 21 (1978): 97–115.

A NT Example

Adams also uses the example of Philippians 2:1-11. Most often, when this passage is expounded, the deity and incarnation of Christ is presented as the central *purpose* of the passage—but is it?

The deity and incarnation of Christ certainly are in there, but they serve to illustrate Paul's larger point: unity within the congregation. Adams explains:

> The Philippian church was split by two quarreling women, Euodious and Syntyche (cf. 4:2-3). Before confronting this division head-on, Paul laid a groundwork for such a discussion by writing about unity and how to attain it.... Paul taught that concern for others would bring unity. Then he gives us the prime example of One who did just that: Jesus Christ.... Certainly this section, containing some of the highest doctrinal teaching regarding the *deity* and incarnation of Christ presents truth (doctrine) *applied*. Paul's concern is not to teach doctrine as such. But he does teach it—*for a purpose*. He wants believers to adopt the same attitude ("mind") that Christ had.[5]

---

[5] Adams, *Truth Applied*, 36 (emphasis original).

For Example...

I prepared a sermon from Romans 3:9-18 recently. I wrote 2 different sentences at the top of my sermon.

- The author's intent: Paul proved to Jews, from their OT, that human beings are entirely corrupt.

- The timeless principle: Every human being is enslaved under sin's corruptive power.

Try It

Look at your preaching text this week. Write out a past-tense sentence (18 words or less) of what the author meant *then*. Next, write-out a present tense sentence (18 words or less) of the *timeless principle now*. That *timeless principle*, which is grounded in the author's original intent, should shape and guide the sermon. To that, we shall turn next.

20

"See Spot Run" & the Sufficiency of Scripture

The first sentence I remember reading as a child was, "See Spot run." The picture book indicated Spot was a dog. *See Spot run*. What does that even mean?

1. [You] see Spot run.
2. *See* Spot run.
3. See *Spot* run.
4. See Spot *run*.

Does it mean "I see the dog run" or "I need to run from the dog" or "the dog needs to run" or what? It depends on the author's *emphasis*.

No preaching textbook I've read deals substantively with the notion of *emphasis*. Yet, from my vantage point, it is the greatest weakness in preaching today, even among expositors.

The Problem

We tend to direct our preaching toward what our culture needs to hear, to what our congregation needs to hear, or as a reaction to current events. This is not wrong unless we begin to tailor the *emphasis* of God's dictates to address that culture, need, or event. In doing so, we inherently deny (or at least weaken) the sufficiency of Scripture we claim to uphold. If you write a message to someone, you arrange it in such a way that you want certain things emphasized more than others. When others alter your *emphasis*, they can alter your meaning.

We often take for granted the level of care and detail God took in bringing His Scripture into existence. He carefully selected His human authors. He brought them into the world in specific places and at strategic times. He raised them up, each one differently, giving them unique experiences: Paul had world-class education and training; Peter and John were fishermen; Amos was a shepherd and a keeper of fig trees; Moses was royal turned shepherd; David was a shepherd turned royal. It is a remarkable collection of authors.

God used each one's historical context, personality, and life experiences to reveal Himself to mankind. When you think about all of this detail and specificity, do you think God was any less careful or less intentional in how

"See Spot Run" & the Sufficiency of Scripture

He arranged the sentences and paragraphs He guided them to write down?

Authorial Emphasis

What do we mean by *"emphasis?"* Emphasis is the degree of attention that should be paid to the meaning and sub-meanings of an author within the sermon event.[1] We make that determination by asking three questions:

1. What "single meaning" is the human author conveying in this thought-unit?
2. What "sub-meanings" (sub-points) feed into that single meaning?
3. How much weight (emphasis) do we give to each one?

E. D. Hirsch wrote a classic book on authorial intent called *Validity in Interpretation*. He argues the only valid interpretation is the author's original meaning. He issued a warning that nearly everyone missed: a different set of emphases can change the author's meaning. For instance, we can extract and explode a sub-point and give it so much weight that it dominates the author's main point. In

---

[1] This is my rewording of the definition provided by E. D. Hirsch, *Validity in Interpretation*, (New Haven: Yale University Press, 1967), 99.

doing so, we have changed the author's emphasis; and that, in turn, has altered his meaning. That chain of events has a weakening effect on the sufficiency of Scripture.

Great Commission Example

The Great Commission in Matthew 28:18-20 is a clear example of this: "Go ye therefore and make disciples..." Most often, when you hear this preached, the *emphasis* is on the word, "Go" (indeed, I once met a man in seminary nobly named, "Go-ye," in honor of this verse—one of my favorite names!). The thrust of the sermon—almost always—is on "going" with the gospel—evangelism and missions.

Yet, a closer study reveals something else at play. "Going" is not the *emphasis* of the passage at all. The main verb in Greek is: "make disciples." Therefore, the *emphasis* of the passage is: "Make disciples." All the other actions in the passage are participles. As such, they are subordinate to the controlling verb. Thus, "make disciples" is the main verb (main point). "Going," "baptizing," and "teaching" are under the main verb's authority (sub-points). This should be reflected in our homiletics (sermon/teaching outline or presentation).

Extracting a sub-point like, "going," and making it dominate the main point changes the author's meaning entirely. And why arbitrarily extract and explode "go" instead of "baptize" or "teaching" anyway? All are participles of equal force. Likely, we do so because in English (and in Greek) that word is placed first in the sentence. Yet, in doing so, we inadvertently change the biblical author's emphasis from "discipleship" to "evangelism."

A Quick Thought

You never know how the Spirit will work when you honor His *emphasis*. A couple once joined our congregation and became solid members. Later, the husband told me one reason they joined was because of the Great Commission sermon. It was the first time he'd ever heard that passage preached in a way which honored and preserved the way God wrote it.

Your sermon should honor the emphases of the biblical author. Try it, trust it, and watch what God does with it!

21

The Greatest Problem in Preaching Today

Earlier I stated I've never seen a preaching textbook deal with *authorial emphasis* in a substantial way. I'd like to explore that a bit more thoroughly. My earlier chapter gave the practical implications (which is what most people are interested in). Yet, we need to understand "why" we believe it for it to become convictional. What follows offers some academic girth to the importance of *authorial emphasis*.

Why does this even matter? In short, it matters because our defense of *authorial emphasis* is at one and the same time a defense of authorial intent, objective truth, and ultimately the sufficiency of Scripture. It will not do for ministers of the gospel to proclaim the sufficiency of Scripture but then deny it in their homiletics (sermon execution).

New Criticism

The academic world of literary theory often seeps down from the ivory tower into the pulpits. Whether you knew it or not, we are coming off the heels of a literary theory that dominated the twentieth century: New Criticism. It has permeated into our own thinking more than we realize. T. S. Eliot was, perhaps, its most recognizable spokesman.

New Criticism sought to eliminate from the interpretive process both the reader's subjective response (which we applaud) and the author's intent (which we decry) by analyzing the text as its own, autonomous entity. All else—historical context, cultural context, the issues at hand that provoked the writing in the first place—must be carved-out so the bare text stands alone. Then, and only then, can the grammatical and syntactical structures be analyzed free from bias—even the original writer's bias. They called this the "text only" ethic in all its purity.

They famously chimed, "A poem should not 'mean,' but 'be;'" and gloried in what they called "exciting new voices" a text can evoke. Why? Because no longer was a text's meaning limited to the author's intention; now, a self-contained text is pregnant with "possible meanings," as many as the grammatical and syntactical structures will yield. The irony is this: they imposed on others this "text only" approach, but they expected others to read their writings strictly according to what they, the author, intended. A classic case of "It applies to thee but not to me."

This literary theory filtered down into Christian preaching, as "textual preaching" was pushed even in seminaries. They encouraged students to set aside the biblical author, his historical context, his cultural context, etc., and examine the self-contained text. "After all," they opined, "the actual words are God-breathed (2 Tim 3:16), not the contextual issues."

While we applaud this strong concentration on the biblical text, we refuse to sever the text from the biblical author's original intention. It is intellectually dishonest to do so. Indeed, it amounts to the theft of the biblical author's intellectual property. As you can see, the battle for objective truth was slipping down the pathway to full-blown Postmodernism (no objective truth)—the wild, wild west of literary theory. A society in which every person has their own version of truth.

Relative Emphasis

Into this state of confusion stepped a man of clarity: E. D. Hirsch. Hirsch, who taught literary criticism at Yale and later at the University of Virginia, recognized where this was headed. He challenged the New Critics with this premise: A text means what an author wills it to mean: nothing more, nothing less.

His seminal book on authorial intent was published in 1967, *Validity in Interpretation*. Hirsch recognized that the author—not the text—controls the grammatical and syntactical structures. His quarrel with the New Critics centered on the *relative emphasis* of an author. He recognized that *relative emphasis* naturally accompanies an "implication" (sub-meaning) of the author's verbal meaning (main proposition). Hirsch defines emphasis as, "the relative degree of attention that should be paid to an implication."[1]

The *relative emphasis* of an implication is pivotal because a wrong emphasis can produce a wrong meaning. Hirsch explains, "A different system of emphases gives a different meaning both to a temporal sequence and to a spatial configuration, and obviously when the object of interpretation is a mute text, the problem of getting its emphases right is particularly difficult."[2] Simply put,

---

[1] E. D. Hirsch, *Validity in Interpretation* (Yale University Press: 1967).

[2] Hirsch, *Validity in Interpretation*, 99. In an unnecessary concession (*Aims of Interpretation* (Chicago: University of Chicago Press, 1976), 79-80), Hirsch later enlarged "meaning" to "simply meaning-for-an-interpreter" instead of clarifying that "meaning" is always a return to the text. Along with Kaiser ("The Current Crisis in Exegesis and the Apostolic Use of Deuteronomy 25:4 in 1 Corinthians 9:8-10," *JETS* 21 (1978): 4), we must "applaud Hirsch for his earlier distinction between 'meaning' and 'significance,'" but not "follow his most recent concession and thereby abandon the principle that 'meaning' is a

Hirsch says to emphasize an implication more or less than did the author can alter the author's meaning. He famously wrote:

> How much emphasis should an implication receive? The straightforward answer is, "Just as much relative emphasis as the author willed it to receive." However, we all know that this answer has to be recast in terms of sharable conventions, since we have no direct access to the author's mind. . . . To determine relative emphasis, therefore, we must have reference to something else that makes the function important, and this something lies at the heart of what genre is. The unifying and controlling idea in any type of utterance, any genre, is the idea of purpose.[3]

What Hirsch correctly saw is this: The larger, single purpose of an author's writing (Hirsch names this the "intrinsic genre") must govern the amount of emphases given to each of its parts. Therefore, we must prioritize and preserve the main proposition and any sub-propositions ("implications," as Hirsch calls them) the author conveys. *Relative emphasis* is not only crucial to meaning (perhaps

---

return to what the author intended to say by his use of words in a particular text."

[3] Hirsch, *Validity in Interpretation*, 99.

it is the most crucial and problematic element of all), it is also highly restrictive; it excludes alternatives.[4]

I know this is rather technical, but it has massive implications on Christian preaching (and on truth in general). When two Bible interpreters approach a text with different emphases, then at least one of the interpretations must be wrong. The conclusion is obvious: to over or under emphasize an implication is to miss the sufficiency of the author's intent. Or, to state it positively, one must affirm the proper emphasis of the biblical author's implications in order to affirm entirely the author's willed meaning. You don't need my help to trace-out the consequences this has on the sufficiency of Scripture. Hirsch concludes, "The principle by which we can discover whether an implication belongs to a meaning turns out to be the concept of intrinsic genre."[5] Accordingly, the following two concepts we centered on earlier are critical: (1) the correct controlling purpose of an author's writing and (2) the correct *relative emphases* that feed that controlling purpose.

Relative emphasis often is demeaned or rejected entirely today, even among faithful expositors. In practice, the relics of New Criticism still reside in our homiletics. We often get the *authorial emphasis* right in our study (our hermeneutics). However, somehow we disconnect it from

---

[4] Hirsch, *Validity in Interpretation*, 230.
[5] Hirsch, *Validity in Interpretation*, 89–90.

The Greatest Problem in Preaching Today

our preaching (our homiletics). This is why *relative emphasis* represents the greatest problem facing Christian preaching today. I shall get to the practical implications (and correction) of this problem next.

22

The Danger of Exemplarist Preaching

Recently, I came across a sermon from John 19:26-27: "Seven Ways to Love Your Mother." Sounds great, but is this what the Apostle John meant when he wrote the account of Jesus hanging on the cross? This is an example of "exemplarist preaching," which ignores the all-important *relative emphasis* of the biblical author.

Exemplarist Tendencies

Sidney Greidanus offers the most extensive treatment I've found of exemplarist preaching.[1] He explains: "[P]reachers, in preaching historical texts, would display the person mentioned in the texts as models to be imitated, as examples to be followed—hence the term

---

[1] See Greidanus, *Sola Scriptura: Problems and Principles in Preaching Historical Texts* (Grand Rapids: Eedmans, 1999), 1-113.

'exemplary preaching.'"[2] Greidanus later asserts that "the redemptive-historical side claims that this is not only an illegitimate use of the preaching text but also a degradation of redemptive history to the level of 'profane' history."[3] His argument (rightly) suggests "exemplarist" sermons deny (or degrade) the redemptive-historical nature of historical texts, and in doing so, undermine the sufficiency of Scripture.

Practically speaking, preachers often lift a biblical character from a historical text and build the sermon around him/her. This presents the historical text not so much as a "fact" of history, but as a contemporary parable or allegory.[4] Greidanus's objection is this: "If the text is historical, it will call for a historical method of interpretation which accounts for its historical (factual) character at every step of the interpretive process."[5] In other words, the text must be taken according to its nature and not merely as a contemporary parable. Otherwise, the uniqueness (or the factual essence) of the text is

---

[2] Greidanus, *Sola Scriptura*, 8. Greidanus also deals with texts that allegedly legitimize exemplary preaching: (1) 1 Corinthians 10; (2) Hebrews 11; and (3) James 5:16-18 (see 113-19). Greidanus maintains the biblical author is not exegeting in those text. Rather, he is merely using examples as illustration, "[T]he fact that one can use an element in a text as an illustration does not mean that that illustration is the specific intent of the text" (119).

[3] Greidanus, *Sola Scriptura*, 59.

[4] Greidanus, *Sola Scriptura*, 61.

[5] Greidanus, *Sola Scriptura*, 62.

The Danger of Exemplarist Preaching

overlooked. Greidanus offers a solution: Expound the person (or characteristic, virtue, moral, etc.) within the redemptive-historical framework (i.e., the larger story of the Bible). That way, the historical nature and purpose of the text is preserved *and* the contemporary audience appreciates the relevance of the text.

We agree with Greidanus's conclusion, but for a slightly different reason. His argument concentrates on exemplary sermons and their negative relationship to the redemptive-historical framework (important as that may be). The more critical concern is in their negative relationship to the biblical author's original intent. Did the biblical author intend for the historical text to be interpreted in an exemplary fashion?

Exemplarist sermons "will preach," as they say in seminary. People love them. However, they often breed even greater problems. What if the examples simply don't fit our situation today; the historical gap defies all attempts to apply them directly; or, there is still too much historical debris clinging to the examples?

In such cases, who gives the preacher the authority to lift a certain element from a text and preach it in isolation to the other elements surrounding it? Certainly, the biblical author did not. If not he, then who?

It is admirable to see preachers who genuinely desire to connect the gospel with the modern audience. Yet, in his zeal to connect, the exemplary preacher does violence to the text by "de-historicizing" certain of its elements. This attempt to gain the contemporary man's ear is a homiletical (i.e., presentation) short-cut that works its way back into the hermeneutical (i.e., interpretation) process.

The Danger

This is a monster problem plaguing preaching today. Preachers disregard God's intent as revealed by His biblical authors in order to gain a hearing. "What does it matter," they object, "so long as I'm preaching biblical truth?" Yet, we must keep asking, "Whose truth? If the single truth-intention of the biblical author is not the objective measure, then who determines truth?" Their position is an "ends justifies the means" approach, which does serious damage to the sufficiency of Scripture. Our earlier survey of Christian preaching shows, inevitably, it is a slippery slope into eventual heresy.

The concern rests in the effects of the exemplary tendencies on the single truth-intention of the author. Haddon Robinson agrees, and he turns the discussion back where it belongs: to the biblical author's single truth-intention. Robinson asserts:

> A less obvious but just as harmful way of ignoring the purpose of a biblical author lies in the common practice of employing the historical narratives as case

The Danger of Exemplarist Preaching

studies in morals, virtues, or spiritual struggles. In such sermons the camaraderie between David and Jonathan models an ideal friendship which all Christians should imitate; the conversation of Jesus with the woman at the well provides lessons on personal evangelism; the story of Ruth and Naomi turns into an example of how Christians should relate to their in-laws; Jacob's struggles at Peniel demonstrates how one must wrestle with God for blessing; Nehemiah becomes a case book for leadership. What is not asked in these sermons is whether the biblical writer intended for these histories to be used in this manner.[6]

Robinson uses the term "ignore," and rightly so. Exemplary tendencies ignore certain foundational tenants of the sufficiency of Scripture. They lift an "atom" from a text and treat it as an individual thought-unit (my next chapter will discuss "atomistic" preaching).

Closing Thought

To take a text and disregard the purpose of its originator denies the verbal meaning. Rather, Robinson asserts, "The purpose of the sermon must flow out of the purpose

---

[6] Haddon Robinson, "Homiletics and Hermeneutics," in *Hermeneutics, Inerrancy, and the Bible* (Grand Rapids: Zondervan, 1984): 809.

of the historical narrative."[7] The critical question is not, "Are the assertions of the preacher true?" Typically, they are. The critical question is, "Are the assertions of the preacher honoring the specific truth-claims flowing from the author's intent?" If not, then the preacher would do better to either choose a different text or submit to the assertions of the author in the preaching text under consideration.

Someone might ask, "Why don't preachers just preach the text?" The answer to that question is quite another matter (that might step on a few toes). Some preachers don't know any better. Others desire to say something "fresh," "new," or "profound" to keep the audience's attention. Others reason, "People have heard this preaching text 100 times. I want to give them a different angle they've never considered." Sadly, some simply covet the praises of men. So they inject seemingly profound ideas into the text.

Too often preachers sacrifice the biblical author's *relative emphasis* at the altar of personal admiration. Whether they realize it or not, this downgrades the sufficiency of Scripture and upgrades themselves in its place. This must stop.

---

[7] Robinson, "Homiletics and Hermeneutics": 812.

The Danger of Exemplarist Preaching

Isn't Holy Scripture sufficient? It is, and the *relative emphasis* of the biblical author is what (1) holds us accountable and (2) holds the sufficiency of Scripture intact.

23

The Danger of Atomistic Preaching

My previous chapter suggested the greatest danger in preaching, even among expositors, is not honoring the *relative emphases* of the biblical author. Most often, this occurs when a preacher extracts a "part" of a text and gives it more weight than did the biblical author. Sidney Greidanus calls that "part" an "atom."

Atomistic Tendencies

Atomistic tendencies extract an implication (or sub-meaning or sub-point) of the author and cause it to dominate the author's single verbal meaning. The result becomes an alteration of the author's original meaning. Greidanus calls this the "isolation of certain 'atoms' *within* the text from the inner coherence, the central thrust of the *text*."[1]

---

[1] Greidanus, *Sola Scriptura*, 63 (emphases original).

An "atom" might be a Bible personality's attribute, experience, or behavior which the preacher extracts and expounds as the main emphasis of the message. The problem with this practice is the main thought of the passage is either ignored or reduced to secondary importance. In either case, the verbal meaning becomes different (or other) than that of the biblical author. Greidanus explains:

> Should any of these "atoms" be treated independently in the sermon, the result would be atomism—making absolute that which is a dependent part—and a loss of the central thrust of the text. Should one, for the sake of a unified sermon, place *one* "atom" central, the central thrust is displaced by that which is not central. In either case the meaning of the text will be distorted.[2]

Greidanus claims this tendency produces sermons that become monotonous because they lose the uniqueness of the text.[3] For example, one can preach essentially the same sermon from the "doubt" of John the Baptist (Matt 11:1-6) and the "doubt" of Thomas (John 20:24-29); or, one could apply the "testing" of the faith of Abraham (Gen 22) in the same way as the "testing" of the faith of the Canaanite woman (Matt 15:21ff.).[4] He rightly asserts:

---

[2] Greidanus, *Sola Scriptura*, 64 (emphasis original).
[3] Greidanus, *Sola Scriptura*, 64.
[4] Greidanus, *Sola Scriptura*, 64.

> [T]he "atom" (doubt, testing) is lifted out of its textual (historic) environment into another realm where, though still called "doubt" or "testing," it has lost its unique connections and therefore its special meaning.[5]

The Danger of Atomistic Tendencies

We can reduce the problem of atomistic tendencies to one basic issue: The degree of *relative emphasis* an implication (or sub-meaning) should receive within the sense of the larger whole. The chief concern occurs when the preacher presents an emphasis (or a set of emphases) that is different than the biblical author's, and the interpretation spawns a different meaning. Therefore, we agree with Greidanus's argument. Further, we see no reason why we should limit it to exemplary or biographical tendencies. The argument equally is valid for those sermons which take a sub-point within the verbal meaning and cause it to dominate the central thrust of the sermon. We must never stop asking, "Who gives the preacher the authority to change the King's emphases? Certainly not the King; and if not He, then who?" An "atom," therefore, ought not be limited to a trait, experience, or attribute. We must begin to think of an "atom" as an implication as well.

---

[5] Greidanus, *Sola Scriptura*, 64.

To extract and explode an "implication" to a place of prominence which challenges the biblical author's primary intent distorts the verbal meaning. This inherently corrupts the doctrine of the sufficiency of Scripture.

A Biblical Example

Grant Osborne shows from Philippians 2:2 how the "atom" of "joy" can challenge—and even silence—the real emphasis, which is "harmony." He observes:

> If the subordinate idea is given extensive clarification, it is a sign that the writer considers it to be a major stress. For example, Philippians 2:2 says, "Make my joy complete by being of the same mind, maintaining the same love, united in spirit, intent on one purpose." Obviously, the primary emphasis is not the completion of Paul's joy but the harmony of the Philippian church, developed in four successive subordinate phrases telling the means for bringing Paul greater joy. In the sermon outline, the point would be harmony, not joy.[6]

We often do violence to the biblical author's intent by shifting the emphasis to address a contemporary issue. To

---

[6] Grant Osborne, *Hermeneutical Spiral* (Downer's Grove, IL: IVP Academic, 2006), 32.

present "joy" as the primary emphasis of Philippians 2:2 does not do justice to the meaning Paul communicates. In fact, it conveys a different meaning (even if a true one) altogether.

Implications on the Sufficiency of Scripture

Typically, preachers will take a text such as the one mentioned by Osborne and see many elements ("atoms") in that text from which to construct sermons. This approach relies a little on the truth of Scripture and a lot on human ingenuity—a dangerous game when handling divine truth. Greidanus astutely observes the "multitude of directions the application could take if the text is seen as a number of elements."[7] He teases-out the impact on the doctrine of the sufficiency of Scripture:

> One could preach on all these (and more) elements in the text; he would not be telling falsehoods, but he would *neglect* the revelation in this particular text. For these individual elements can be found in many another text.... But the fact that one can use an element in a text as an illustration does not mean that that illustration is the "specific intent of the text."

---

[7]Greidanus, *Sola Scriptura*, 119.

It's not so much that the preacher is denying truth or preaching falsehoods (it's more subtle than that). Rather, he implicitly (and typically unknowingly) thinks he can arrange it better by shifting the weight of God's *relative emphases*. God breathed out Scripture precisely as He saw fit. As one African-American preacher in my area astutely observed, "God don't need no help from nobody!" We agree.

Kevin Vanhoozer applies this principle to "proof-texting" as well:

> We may note in passing that the tendency among theological conservatives to offer "proof texts"—a method of abstracting individual statements from their larger literary context—is every bit as detrimental to understanding the literary act as a whole as is form criticism. Though they may inhabit different ends of the theological spectrum and though their doctrines of Scripture may be vastly different, the interpretive practice of both form critics and theological conservatives is equally atomistic, equally unlettered—equally capable of short-circuiting the process of interpretation.[8]

---

[8] Vanhoozer, *Is There Meaning in this Text?* (Grand Rapids: Eerdmans), 337.

The Danger of Atomistic Preaching

A more scripturally sufficient practice is this: Simply retain the biblical author's *relative emphases*. Walt Kaiser advises:

> Time and again the exegete may be saved from would-be disaster and the perils of subjectivism by relying on the text's own pattern of emphasis as it is often indicated by some stylistic, grammatical, or rhetorical device that supplies the authoritative basis for principlizing that text."[9]

The pattern of emphasis dictated by the text keeps verbal meaning in its rightful and preeminent position in the interpretive process. All of this is not to say that implications ought not be expounded; indeed, they should. However, implications must remain submissive to the author's intent—and to the degree that the original author wills them. Otherwise, we comprise the sufficiency of Scripture since the biblical author's emphases are, in fact, God's emphases.

---

[9] Kaiser, *Toward an Exegetical Theology*, 156.

24

The Danger of Biographical Sermons

Everyone loves a good biography. Something about reading of the trials and triumphs of others captures our imagination. Biographical lectures on the Protestant Reformers by the likes of John MacArthur, Steve Lawson, and others have challenged and deepened my faith tremendously. Indeed, I discovered several biographies on William Tyndale, the first person to translate the NT into English from the Greek manuscripts. I was so impressed by his heroic life, I named my second son, Titus Tyndale Thornton. Biographies are a wonderful source of spiritual edification. Before we leave the topic of the *relative emphasis* of the biblical author, though, I should mention one other danger: biographical sermons.

Biographical Preaching

Biographical preaching is lifting an individual person from Holy Scripture and constructing a sermon from that individual's life experience. Once again, Sidney Greidanus is one of the few who have stopped to consider the implications this might have on the doctrine of the sufficiency of Scripture. His work in this area is exceptional.[1]

The Danger of Biographical Sermons

The danger of biographical sermons is they typically "are in essence *anthropocentric*" (i.e., man-centered).[2] He explains:

> The *sola Scriptura*, so ardently confessed in theory, barely functions in the practice of exemplary preaching: one hardly needs the Bible for exemplary sermons. Ironically, the exemplary preacher, earnestly toiling to portray the man in the text in his personal struggles, therewith the better to draw a line to the man in the pew, could, methodologically, have saved himself the trouble and sketched merely the man in the pew, for, motivated by the search for analogy (relevance), he loses precisely that distinctiveness which occasioned the appearance in the Bible of man in the text.[3]

---

[1] See his book, *Sola Scriptura*.
[2] Greidanus, *Sola Scriptura*, 66–67.
[3] Greidanus, *Sola Scriptura*, 70.

The Danger of Biographical Sermons

Biographical sermons, while true, typically don't reflect the biblical author's single truth-intention. This has implications on the sufficiency of Scripture that almost no one wants to talk about.

Greidanus suggests preachers or teachers who desire to be Christocentric in their preaching often end up with a Bible character as central.[4] He argues biographical sermons misjudge the historical text by severing a character from his redemptive-historical place in Scripture. In so doing, they "dishonor" Scripture.[5] He makes this observation, "Biographical preaching is anthropocentric, however, and if one wants to preach on the lives of men, Scripture, in effect, is optional."[6] The biographical character is extracted from the total context of redemptive history through fragmentary interpretation (i.e., the shattering of redemptive history into smaller, individual histories), thereby leaving only (1) the character and (2) an unhistorical text. When the biblical character is left all by himself in a non-historical genre, the authority of Scripture recedes. At that point, Greidanus correctly notes, Abraham's virtues (or vices) may just as well be preached from the Koran as the Bible.[7]

---

[4] Greidanus, *Sola Scriptura*, 67.
[5] Greidanus, *Sola Scriptura*, 69.
[6] Greidanus, *Sola Scriptura*, 85.
[7] Greidanus, *Sola Scriptura*, 69.

A Closing Thought

Again, we agree with Greidanus's conclusion, but for a different reason. The crux of the issue is not the disconnection of the text from redemptive history (although, that is important). Rather, the critical issue is the disconnection of the text from the author's intent. As always, we ask, "Did the author intend for the preaching text to be interpreted biographically?" If not, then why do it? Any answer to the latter question will emerge from a man-centered desire (even if well-intended). That biographical sermon likely represents a denial of the sufficiency of Scripture (which is why no one wants to talk about this).

Most of us have preached a biographical sermon or two (or more!). We all know God can take even an imperfect methodology and use it for good. In the future, though, it is worth stopping to consider, "What implications does this methodology have on the sufficiency of Scripture? Am I setting a precedent that takes a small step away from the biblical author's single meaning? If the biblical author didn't intend this pericope as a biography, am I comfortable departing from his intent?" These hard questions, but they are worth exploring.

Application

25

Point-to-Point Application

Often, biblical authority is lost in the transition from the biblical text to the contemporary application. Somewhere in that gap, we (sometimes) sever ties to the author's intent and forsake all biblical authority. It is in the sermon's application that we often hear the commandments of men preached as the doctrines of God. In fact, the first part of the Sermon on the Mount, largely, was a primer in correct application: "You have heard that it was said . . . but I say to you." The implication: if the biblical author controls his meaning (and he does), then he also controls the application of his meaning. What follows will be devoted to correcting this application problem, a problem few even know exists.

Allow the Biblical Text to Drive the Application

Kaiser correctly diagnosed the problem: when an application has only a superficial connection to the author's verbal meaning, then it must be judged as a wrong application.[1] We explored this "bridging the gap" concept in a previous chapter, but now we must go further.

We must discover the genuine relationship(s) between the biblical author's *"single meaning"* and its abiding *"significance."* These parameters remain in place:

1. Every preaching-text has a *"single meaning"*; therefore,

2. Every preaching-text has a *"timeless principle"*; however,

3. That *"timeless principle"* can apply to multiple situations.

In moving from the biblical author's *"single meaning"* to the *"specific application"* of his meaning, we must find legitimate applicatory relationships between the two. The following are some points of consideration.

---

[1] Walter C. Kaiser, Jr., "Inner Biblical Exegesis as a Model for Bridging the 'Then' and 'Now' Gap: Hos 12:1-6," *JETS* 28 (Mar 1985): 34.

Considerations in Point-to-Point Application

1. Make sure the text's purpose and application match.

2. Make sure the text's emphasis approximates the contemporary situation's emphasis.

3. Look for "commonalities" between the original audience and the contemporary one.[2]

    a. Do both audiences belong to the universal church?

    b. Do both share things such as God's attributes, God's law, etc.?

    c. Do both share the expectation that God's Word is relevant today?

    d. Do both share the idea that the OT provides background to NT?

4. Be aware of unique cultural situations which don't apply today.

5. Be cognizant of when the biblical author is addressing/correcting a problem.

---

[2] See Ramesh Richard, "Methodological Proposals for Scripture Relevance: Part 3: Application Theory in Relation to the New Testament," *BSac* 143 (1986): 208–15.

6. Be mindful of the continuity and discontinuity between OT Israel and the NT church.
7. Make certain you can trace-back any application directly to the text. If you have to over-explain it, a legitimate relationship likely doesn't exist between the text and your application.

Point-to-Point Example: 1 Corinthians 9:7–11

Earlier, we examined how the Apostle Paul applied Deuteronomy 25:4 ("muzzling the ox") in 1 Corinthians 9:7–11. Deuteronomy 24–25 memorialized a list of civil laws illustrating the moral way God would have His people behave. Paul recognized Deuteronomy 25:4 establishes a *"timeless principle."* In the original context, some of the crop was given to feed the ox who performed the labor. The *"timeless principle"* is this: if animals deserve to be compensated for their labors, people deserve to be compensated for their labors, too. Paul transferred that to his present-day audience, "The plowman should plow in hope . . . of sharing in the crop" (1 Cor 9:10).

The specific application Paul made was to gospel preachers: "In the same way, the Lord commanded that those who proclaim the gospel should get their living by the gospel" (1 Cor 9:14).

Point-to-Point Application

Let's track the legitimate relationship between the single meaning of Moses and the application of Paul.

Single Meaning: The ox should get food from those who benefit from his labors.

The Timeless Principle: People should be compensated from those who benefit from his labors.

Paul's Specific Application: Gospel ministers should be provided for by those who benefit from their labors.

The *"timeless principle"* is single, but it may be applied to other areas as well. If you are a business owner, provide for your employees who labor on your behalf; if someone does repair work on your home, provide fairly for him/her—even generously—if you are able; if someone teaches your children, provide for them to the extent you can. In short, do unto others as you would have done unto you.

Conclusion

One great tragedy in preaching is when our application has only a loose connection to the biblical text—or worse, an illegitimate one. Weak applicatory connections reduce the gospel preacher to nothing more than a motivational speaker. This happens all too often. Ground your application in solid, biblical authority. Then, watch the Spirit use it to change men's hearts.

26

Abstraction

If we truly hold to the sufficiency of Scripture, then we must discover the legitimate applicatory relationships, correspondences, or common elements between the biblical text and the contemporary setting. We shall look at three (of the few) men who have probed these matters: Jay E. Adams, Ramesh Richard, and Walt Kaiser. They have similar processes, but each has its own nuances and terminology: Adams calls it abstraction;[1] Richard calls it extrapolation;[2] and Kaiser calls it principlization.[3] Grasping these concepts will aid in discovering legitimate, author-driven applications grounded in strong, biblical authority.

---

[1] Jay E. Adams, *Truth Applied: Application in Preaching* (Grand Rapids: Zondervan, 1990), 33-55; Adams, *Preaching with Purpose*, (Grand Rapids: Zondervan, 1982), 16-33, 131-45.

[2] Ramesh Richard's thoughtful four-part series titled, "Methodological Proposals for Scripture Relevance" in *BSac* 143 (1986), 14-25, 123-33, 205-17, 302-13.

[3] Kaiser, *Toward an Exegetical Theology*, 149-60; and "Inner Biblical Exegesis as a Model for Bridging the 'Then' and 'Now' Gap: Hosea 12:1-6," *JETS* 28 (Mar 1985), 33-36, 43-46.

Tether the Verbal Meaning to the *Telos*

Let's start with Adams. Adams is concerned, first, with finding the single purpose of the preaching text, which he calls the *telos*. The *telos* is the primary purpose of the text and corresponds with what we call the *"timeless principle."* He rightly observes:

> [Much] preaching has failed because God's *telos* (or purpose) in the preaching passage has been ignored by preachers who, instead, use it for their own purposes, thereby misusing it and losing the force of the passage.[4]

It is in our application that we often, inadvertently, deny the sufficiency of Scripture. This is cause for concern. Merely attaching vague similarities between the text's *telos* (purpose) and the modern audience is insufficient.[5] Rather, the primary thrust of the preaching passage must match the primary thrust of the application.

For example, we mentioned earlier how Adams applies this concept to Philippians 1:27–2:13. Now, watch

---

[4] Adams, *Truth Applied*, 36

[5] Adams, *Preaching with Purpose*, 136, articulates, "Discovering similarities is not enough; the similarities that count are those which are basic, not those which are secondary. To find a correlation between superficial factors is to allow one's self to be deflected from the *telic* thrust of a preaching portion to something that was not intended at all. ... The task, then, is to find the constant, or basic thrust in each circumstance to which God's authoritative Word speaks."

how he aligns the "purpose" of the text with its "application:"

> The Philippian church was split by two quarreling women, Euodious and Syntyche (cf. 4:2-3). Before confronting this division head-on, Paul laid a groundwork for such a discussion by writing about unity and how to attain it.... Paul taught that concern for others would bring unity. Then he gives us the prime example of One who did just that: Jesus Christ.... Certainly this section, containing some of the highest doctrinal teaching regarding the *deity* and incarnation of Christ presents truth (doctrine) *applied*. Paul's concern is not to teach doctrine as such. But he does teach it—*for a purpose*. He wants believers to adopt the same attitude ("mind") that Christ had.[6]

Many may identify the deity and incarnation of Christ as the purpose of this passage, but Adams correctly ascertains: Paul set forth Christ (and his embodiment of these doctrinal truths) as an illustration of the larger point he was making regarding unity within the church. Adams is correct: we must tether the verbal meaning to the *telos*.

---

[6] Adams, *Truth Applied*, 36.

Tether the *Telos* to the Specific Application

Next, Adams traces the legitimate applicational correspondences through a method he calls "abstraction." Abstraction lifts the *telos* (or, "*timeless principle,*" as we call it) from the biblical passage. Then, he applies it to a contemporary context. The preacher must do two things: (1) abstract the timeless principle from the preaching text and (2) abstract the elements in the preaching-text that approximate the contemporary situation.[7] Regarding the latter, Adams advises, "When the elements in both the biblical and the contemporary situations match, the abstracted principle may be reapplied."[8] The following questions, which we set forth in an earlier chapter, help connect the dots between the timeless principle and the present-day context. A healthy exercise is to write-out the answer to these questions as you prepare each sermon/lesson:

1. What is the *telos* of the preaching portion? Is that also the *telos* of your sermon?

2. In what sort of situation does the *telos* occur? What was going on? To what is it addressed?

---

[7] Adams, *Truth Applied*, 47–48.
[8] Adams, *Truth Applied*, 48.

Abstraction

3. In the passage who is doing what about the situation?

    a. to understand it?

    b. to change it?

    c. to complicate it?

4. How does God view the situation?
5. Is He pleased with it?
6. Is He displeased with it?
7. What response does He require?[9]

This tethers the *telos* to the specific application. The value of this exercise is this: It begins eliminating illegitimate applicatory relationships that deny the sufficiency of the biblical author's intent. It preserves the biblical author's prerogative to reach from the grave into the present-day life. Since Scripture is "breathed-out by God" (2 Tim. 3:16), God took this into account when He brought the text into existence through His human author.

Key Points

Two key points to glean from Adams:

---

[9] Adams, *Truth Applied*, 54.

1. The *telos* of the text and the *telos* of the message must match.
2. The application of a passage must establish legitimate common elements—not mere similarities—between the original setting and the contemporary one.

Adams's controls are beneficial, albeit broad. Therefore, we shall tighten the screws further by examining Ramesh Richard's work next.

27

Extrapolation

We've been exploring how to navigate through the "gap" between what the biblical text meant "then" and how it applies "now." Ramesh Richard's contribution, which he calls, "extrapolation," actually implies there are two "gaps." It might be helpful to name them the "A" gap (the space between the verbal meaning and the "*timeless principle*") and the "B" gap (the space between the "*timeless principle*" and the proper application). Those are my designations, not Richard's, but they are true to his process. Let's explore his work.

First, Extrapolate the Verbal Meaning

Richard holds that extrapolation is a "constituent" of meaning.[1] He explains, "Extrapolation unpacks linguistic

---

[1] Richard, "Methodological Proposals for Scripture Relevance: Part 2: Levels of Biblical Meaning," 126, declares, "[T]here is a field of meaning around each statement. This field of meaning is on three levels: *statement, implication,* and *extrapolation.*" For Richard, "extrapolation" brings the exegete to the point where the applicatory process can begin and is primarily concerned with this question: What would the author have meant if he wrote this text today? Application, on the other hand, is "the bridge between meaning and the present" (129).

phenomena but also brings biblical meaning to the point where application can be made and significance drawn. However, extrapolation is not application."[2] We prefer to keep extrapolation separate from meaning because the process of extrapolation begins once the meaning already has been determined. Blending the two creates unnecessary confusion, causing more problems than it solves. Nevertheless, Richard's excellent work has much to offer to the discussion on proper application.

Richard arrives at what we call *"the timeless principle"* through a sequence of steps. First, he deciphers the verbal meaning. Second, he bridges the "A" gap by extrapolating the meaning. This leads him to the *"the timeless principle."*[3] Finally, he steps in the "B" gap to bridge the *"timeless principle"* to some aspect of life (we call this "application").[4]

---

[2] Richard, "Levels of Biblical Meaning," 128-29.

[3] Richard distinguishes between the "application" and "significance." The "application process" is what happens in the "A" gap and seems to include extrapolation; the "significance" is what happens in the "B" gap; namely, how the application relates to the contemporary situation. Kaiser uses these terms in the exact opposite way. For Kaiser, "significance" corresponds to what we call the "timeless principle;" and "application" corresponds to what most people think as specific present-day "uses." The confusion of terms/semantic is why we opted for the much simpler: *verbal meaning – timeless principle – present-day application*. Richard's definitions are similar to those of Robert H. Stein, "An Author-Oriented Approach to Hermeneutics," *JETS* 44 (2001): 461. Stein includes application as a part of meaning but keeps significance distinct.

[4] See Richard, "Levels of Biblical Meaning," 126-31, and "Methodological Proposals for Scripture Relevance: Part 3: Application Theory in Relation to the New Testament," 206-15. Richard's terminology is

Extrapolation

Then, Follow the Stepping-Stones

Once the author's intent has been ascertained, Richard points us to some stepping-stones (my term, not his) that emerge to help us bridge the gap. Most of his work concentrates on the "A" gap between the ancient text and the *"timeless principle."*

Old Testament Stepping-Stones

Regarding Old Testament passages, Richard offers a three-pronged checklist: (1) analyze the theological analogy; (2) consider the theocratic factor; and (3) understand the trans-temporal constants.[5] The first addresses the differences in the old dispensation and the new dispensation.[6] The second speaks both to the *discontinuity* between "then" and "now" (because of God's governance of the church-state nation, Israel) and to the *continuity* (because of God's governance of the church in redemptive history). He suggests both the continuity and the discontinuity should be highlighted during the applicatory process. Of course, this may vary slightly, depending on your

---

slightly different, which can be confusing, but the concepts are the same.

[5] For some examples, see Richard, "Methodological Proposals for Scripture Relevance: Part 4: Application Theory in Relation to the Old Testament," 304–10.

[6] Richard writes from an admittedly dispensational perspective.

systematic framework of theology (covenantal, dispensational, or somewhere in-between). The third has to do with those constants shared by both the people of Israel and the present-day church such as the nature of God, the nature of man, and the nature of salvation.

New Testament Stepping-Stones

Regarding New Testament passages, Richard offers two New Testament criteria as determinants for proper application: (1) audience-referent and (2) audience-trait. The former echoes Jay Adams's emphasis on the *telos* of the passage and need not be rehashed (see our previous chapter). The latter refers to any "commonality" the original audience shares with the contemporary, which include the following three considerations.[7] Richard offers five correspondences between the two audiences: (1) both belong to the universal church; (2) both share trans-temporal constants, such as the nature and attributes of God, the eternal law of God, etc.; (3) both share application-expectation of the biblical writings; (4) both depend upon apostolic authority for guidance; and, (5) both depend on the Old Testament to provide cultural, historical, and

---

[7] Richard, "Application Theory in Relation to the New Testament," 208–15.

theological background for central events and concepts of the New Testament.[8]

First, he distinguishes between "submissional" application (the original audience's mandate to submit to a command) versus "relationship-to-life" application (where the church must apply the principle of the specific command). For example, consider Paul's discussion of women praying with their heads covered (1 Cor 11). "Submissional" application would refer to Paul's original audience submitting to his command. Relationship-to-life application would refer to how the church must apply that command in the contemporary context (see my previous chapter on the subject).

Second, he suggests that, for every passage, there are two foci to the applicational bridge: (1) interpretation of meaning for application and (2) interpretation of application for significance. The former refers to the process of extrapolating the meaning in order to determine the significance (i.e., the first "gap"); the latter refers to the process of applying the significance to a particular situation (i.e., the second "gap").

Lastly, he advocates generalizing time-specific commands.[9] Richard's technical, yet important, work helps us

---

[8] Richard, "Application Theory in Relation to the New Testament," 208-09.

[9] Richard, "Application Theory in Relation to the New Testament," 212-14. He provides eight guidelines: (1) determine the level of abstraction of any moral form in Scripture; (2) be sensitive to historically and

shoot a straighter line between correct verbal meaning and proper application.

Concluding Analysis

The value of Richard's contribution is he offers specific criteria, almost a checklist, we can use as stepping stones between the verbal meaning and the end-user application. Few attempt this. We all would do well to follow these steppingstones before we settle on a specific application.

We appreciate Richard for alerting us to the myriad of issues to consider. However, it seems a little complicated. We are still left wondering how to implement a simple, common-sense approach which ferrets out genuine relationships, correspondences, or common elements between the "then" and "now." Kaiser is one of the few who makes a concerted effort to do so. To him, we shall turn next.

---

culturally unique situations; (3) discern which moral discursive forms speak to ethical action and attitudes; (4) ask, "Are there principles stated explicitly elsewhere in Scripture that are here applied specifically?;" (5) seek for God's purposes and eternal will in Scripture; (6) determine the relationship between the ethical command and the problem that gave rise to it; (7) look for linguistic indicators that define the issue; and, (8) be willing to change one's circumstances in obedience to the normative teaching of Scripture.

28

Principlization

The progression from a biblical author's verbal meaning to a correct application follows this track:

Verbal meaning—("A" gap)—Timeless Principle—("B" gap)—Application

Ramesh Richard's "extrapolation" method largely dealt with what happens in the space we call the "A" gap. Kaiser's "principlization" method largely deals with what happens in the space we call the "B" gap.

Principlization aims to ground any end-user application in the truth-intention of the biblical author. The only legitimate end-user application is found in the biblical author's grammar and syntax. Any application with merely a superficial connection to the author's verbal meaning must be judged as a wrong one.[1] Implementing four homiletical controls will guide us through the "B" gap space. At the least, it will help (1) to eliminate flawed end-user applications and (2) to fix our attention on those legitimate

---

[1] See Kaiser, "Inner Biblical Exegesis . . . ," 34.

correspondences which are grounded in the biblical author's verbal meaning.

Match-up the Subject of the Text and Message

The first control is to make the subject of the *preaching-text* the subject of the *message*. Make certain to: (1) analyze the theme sentences in each paragraph (refer to your hermeneutical study); (2) look for distinctive features in the passage; and (3) study the opening words or headings, which set the stage for how the passage develops.[2]

Match-up the Emphasis of the Text and Message

The second control is to transfer the emphasis of the *preaching-text* to the emphasis of the message. Kaiser highlights two criteria which will govern that transference. First, identify important words/key terms by their frequency/strategic position in the syntactical construction.[3] These often are obvious points the author wishes to

---

[2] See Kaiser, *Toward an Exegetical Theology*, 152–55.
[3] Kaiser, *Toward an Exegetical Theology*, 155.

convey.[4] Second, analyze conjunctives which link sentences. Conjunctives alert us to consequences or reasons the author conveys. For example, Kaiser traces out how a biblical author's emphasis relates to (what we call) the *"timeless principle;"* and ultimately, the end-user application:

> Whenever a series of sentences or clauses is linked together by the same introductory word ("because," "since," "therefore," or the like) it may be possible to organize the message aground these key words. In this case each major point in the sermon will be a development of the subject from the same perspective and angle. For example, if the word *therefore* is sprinkled throughout the paragraphs under investigation, then we may safely make our major points in the sermon a discussion of the *consequences* of the announced subject. Alternatively, if the word *because* recurs frequently, we may develop our message around a series of *reasons*.[5]

---

[4] Kaiser, *Toward an Exegetical Theology*, 156. For instance, in 1 Thessalonians 4:1-8, follow the three infinitival forms in 3b, 4a, and 6a.

[5] Kaiser, *Toward an Exegetical Theology*, 155-56.

Match up the Movements of the Text with the Message

The third control is to mirror the *preaching-text's* main points and sub-points in the *message*. This takes tremendous discipline, as our natural inclination is to get the verbal meaning correct and then apply it as we see fit. No, this is too subjective. Left to ourselves, we tend to gravitate toward applications "related" to the preaching-text but not necessarily "rooted" in it.

Diagramming the text is the safest way to enact this control. If, as Kaiser advises, you reduce every paragraph to a single sentence, then the author's main points should become clear. These theme sentences should be analyzed in relation to the author's larger scope in the preaching-text. Kaiser suggests "weighing each topic sentence against the author's major concern in the whole text under scrutiny."[6]

Once the main points fall into place, any sub-points the author expresses should feed into them. Your sermon/teaching outline should mirror the text in this way. This exercise will anchor your end-user application to the biblical author's syntactical constructions, the latter being the surest source of clues as to how the author intended his text to be applied.

---

[6] Kaiser, *Toward an Exegetical Theology*, 157.

Match up the Theology in the Text to the Message

The final control is to reflect the theology in the *preaching-text* as the theology of the *message*. Two guiding principles must govern this. First, "emerging theology" must take precedence over systematic theology. "Emerging theology" refers only to the biblical revelation the author knew at the time he wrote. Kaiser touts the analogy of antecedent Scripture we spelled out in an earlier chapter. That is, we must never superimpose later revelation (of which the author was unaware) onto the preaching-text. Doing so will distort his verbal meaning, which will distort the end-user application.[7] This is not to say systematic theology is irrelevant. Quite the opposite, which leads us to Kaiser's next guiding principle.

Second, the proper place for systematic theology is in summaries and conclusions.[8] Later revelation should be reserved for summary sections of each main point. This best upholds the sufficiency of each preaching-text. Kaiser's point here is worthy. If this informing theology was what made the text timeless and full of abiding values for the people in that day (and we believe that it was), then could not this same diachronic accumulation of theology provide the same heart of the message for all peoples in all

---

[7] Kaiser, *Toward an Exegetical Theology*, 161.
[8] Kaiser, *Toward an Exegetical Theology*, 161.

times? Yes, for even in the text's historical particularity, it also carried in its very bosom an enduring plan of the everlasting God.[9]

Kaiser seeks to maintain the relation between the biblical author's meaning and its significance to changing contexts. Therefore, legitimate application—first—should reflect the theology in the text at the time it was written; and—second—shed light on any subsequent revelation via conclusions and summary statements. This final control takes into account Richard's "extrapolation" method in a way that harnesses allegorical tendencies where they seem most likely to appear: namely, in the "gaps." Kaiser wisely cautions:

> In the past grids that had been devised outside of the text were dropped in place over the text to yield some theological payload from the Bible.... At best, it restructures the Bible according to one's favorite schema or pet doctrine; but what authority and guidance are left after the text has been treated so subjectively?[10]

Each of these methods—abstraction, extrapolation, and principlization—are helpful in determining correct application. Use all of them as you work your way through

---

[9] Kaiser, *Toward an Exegetical Theology*, 162.
[10] Kaiser, *Toward an Exegetical Theology*, 138.

Principlization

the "gaps." At the end, double-check yourself with a simple, common-sense question: "If the biblical author were standing here today, would he apply it this way?" If not, then neither should we.

29

Reaching from the Grave

Years ago, I worked in a legal office. I wrote the Last Will & Testament for many clients. Some clients had certain assets they wanted to bequest to certain people in certain ways. For example, they might desire a child receives an annual distribution commencing at their eighteenth birthday, provided the child: (1) is a full-time employee; (2) is a full-time student; (3) serves in the military; or (4) serves a charitable organization at least thirty hours a week. We called this "reaching from the grave." Once the testator died, we had an ethical responsibility to follow his/her wishes with integrity.

Pastors have a similar ethical responsibility.[1] This responsibility includes making certain the biblical author's meaning and intended application(s) are preserved. Few

---

[1] The subject of an interpreter's ethical responsibility received some attention years ago, but it has waned. Those who address the issue best are: Kevin Vanhoozer, *Is There Meaning in this Text?* 148–95, 367–452; Timothy Ward, *Word and Supplement: Speech Acts, Biblical Texts, and the Sufficiency of Scripture* (Oxford: University Press, 2002), 94–105 and 137–207; and Nicolas Wolterstorff, *Divine Discourse: Philosophical Reflections on the Claim that God Speaks* (Cambridge: University Press, 1995), 75–94.

(if any) preaching textbooks mention this subject, likely because it limits our freedom to apply passages as *"we"* see fit. Yet, an ethical responsibility resides in the written text and extends to the interpreter.

Most of us have been taken out of context at some point in our life. Karl Barth, after reading a review of one of his own books, felt as though he had been "cannibalized" because his writings were intentionally misrepresented. He wrote to Professor Geoffrey W. Bromiley of Fuller Seminary and refused to answer questions from fundamentalists. He felt they had misrepresented him. Bart quotes an eighteenth-century poem: "There is no true love where one man eats another," and then exclaims, "These fundamentalists want to eat me up."[2] Whether his frustration was justified or not, who among us has not felt similarly?

Would the biblical writers cringe at how we apply their sacred truths? Or, do we even care? Perhaps that is the more relevant question.

Think Through Speech Act Theory

Present-day application(s) call for decisions from the reader. The arguments presented by "Speech Act Theory"

---

[2] See Vanhoozer, *Is There Meaning in this Text?*, 161; see also, Karl Barth, *Letters 1961–1968*, ed. and trans. Geoffrey W. Bromiley (Grand Rapids: Eerdmans, 1971), 7–8.

(i.e., the study of how words relate to intended actions) offer some restraints on a reader's decision-making. Timothy Ward, one of the better (and more understandable writers on the subject, argues that the determinancy of textual meaning controls the determinancy of relationships between author, text, and reader.[3] Without getting too technical, an author's right to determine his meaning is conducted through the illocutionary (i.e., communication) force of his speech act. This illocutionary force—a warning, a promise, a request, etc.—establishes a new ethical relationship between author and reader, which in turn adjudicates the moral responsibilities assigned to each party.[4] Accordingly, Ward concludes, the illocutionary force "protects the identity of each of the three elements, author, text, and reader, from being dissolved into any of the others. In addition, it makes clear the ethical and determinate character of the relationships which exist between authors, texts, and readers."[5] All of this is interesting enough, but what does it mean for pastors?

---

[3] Ward, *Word and Supplement*, 138.
[4] Ward, *Word and Supplement*, 199. Ward remarks, "These moral rights and responsibilities are determinate, and constitute the determinate relationships between author, text, and reader."
[5] Ward, *Word and Supplement*, 205.

Think Through Your Ethical Responsibility

It means we have a solemn, ethical responsibility to the biblical author to stay within the confines of his intended outcome(s). We must honor several virtues of integrity few are willing to consider. Vanhoozer suggests four: (1) honesty; (2) openness; (3) attention; and, (4) obedience.[6]

Honesty acknowledges one's prior experiences, making a genuine effort to lay aside those preunderstandings.

Openness hears the biblical author without prejudice or malice, and it requires a willingness to change.

Attention makes a genuine attempt to explore the details and various levels of the literary act (genre, syntax, word meanings, etc.).

Obedience follows the directions of the text, reading the genre as the author intended it to be read (i.e., reading history as history, apocalyptic as apocalyptic, etc.).

Too often, we violate our ethical responsibilities, and it is our end-user application(s) which implicitly betray us. This must change.

---

[6] Vanhoozer, *Is There Meaning in this Text?*, 376–77.

Concluding Thought

Allegorical tendencies in application are the most difficult aspect of preaching to evaluate. In the leap between the author's verbal meaning and his end-user application(s), we move from dealing with a concrete entity (namely, the text) to an abstract entity (that is, the relationship of that text to changing situations). We can go wayward quickly, often without even realizing it. This is why the previous chapters on abstraction, extrapolation, and principlization are crucial. Yet, even when those procedures remain airtight, we still risk losing biblical authority when we relax our ethical responsibility to the biblical author we claim to represent.

Biblical authors wrote with an eye toward "reaching from the grave." Don't cut off their arm for personal prestige or gain.

Homiletics

30

Sermon Steps

Where do I begin? That was my biggest struggle in preparing a sermon. I'd sit for hours with an open Bible before me, and . . . nothing. I'd know the passage inside and out, but I seemed to have trouble getting the process going: How do I start it? Where do I start it? How do I close it? Sometimes, I'd sit for several hours trying to think of good opening illustration. I wasted much too much time. Hopefully, what follows will spare you such troubles.

At this point, we've looked at hermeneutics and homiletics. Now, we must bring them together in a cogent way which models Nehemiah 8:8: "They read from the Book, from the Law of God, clearly, and they gave the sense, so that the people understood the reading." That is our endgame: that the people understand what God has written.

We suggest reducing all your sweat-work to a single page for clarity. This single page will move deliberately in the following manner:

Biblical Text → Single Meaning → TimelessPrinciple → Major Objective of the Sermon (MOS) → Title → Outline.[1]

Write Down the Single Meaning

First, write down the *single meaning* of the text. Fasol defines the single meaning (he calls it the Central Idea of the Text; or, the CIT) as a "fifteen-to-eighteen-word (maximum) past-tense statement interpreting what the text meant then."[2] In short, this is a concise sentence which memorializes the biblical author's intent. This statement is of utmost importance because the rest of the sermon will take its shape from the single meaning.

Take Mark 9:33-37 as a case study. Our hermeneutical study yields this single meaning: *Jesus taught that greatness came by serving all people, including those who can't help themselves.*

For the listener's clarity, state this sentence somewhere in the sermon, preferably directly before or after

---

[1] I learned this method from Al Fasol in 2001 when he was professor of preaching at Southwestern Baptist Theological Seminary. His invaluable little volume, *Steps to the Sermon*, is an easy-to-follow guide for sermon preparation. See C. Brown, Jr., H. Gordon Clinard, Jesse J. Northcutt, and Al Fasol, *Steps to the Sermon*, rev ed. (Nashville: Broadman & Holman Publishers, 1996).

[2] Al Fasol, *Essentials for Biblical Preaching* (Grand Rapids: Baker Book House, 1989), 56.

reading the passage. This will allow the biblical author to direct the shape and content of the sermon.

State the Timeless Principle

Next, write down the *timeless principle*. Fasol defines the timeless principle (he calls it the thesis) as "a fifteen-to-eighteen-word (maximum) present-tense application of the CIT" [i.e., the single meaning sentence].[3] The timeless principle is the bridge between the ancient text and the contemporary context. It conveys how and/or why the text is relevant today.

Consider Mark 9:33–37. The text yields this timeless principle: *True greatness comes by serving others despite the cost.* Fasol wisely counsels, "A good thesis is timeless and universal."[4] Again, we recommend stating the timeless principle somewhere in the sermon. A logical place to state it is in the introduction when you are making a connection with your audience.

---

[3] Fasol, *Essentials for Biblical Preaching*, 57. CIT = "Central Idea of the Text."

[4] Fasol, *Steps to the Sermon*, 66.

Think Through the Major Objective of the Sermon

Third, write out the *major objective of the sermon (MOS)*. Fasol defines it as "a statement of what the preacher hopes to accomplish with this one message, from this one text, for this one congregation, at this one particular time."[5] Of course, the MOS must emerge from the timeless principle.

Let's say we are called upon to proclaim Mark 9:33–37 to a small, middle-class church in a medium sized city. The MOS might be: *To ignite a passion in Christians for serving others.* A helpful tip: Use a strong verb to capture the listener's attention. It is not necessary to state the MOS outright in the sermon. If you do, the natural place is either in the introduction or the conclusion.

Think of a Sermon Title

Fourth, write out the *sermon's title*. Some like to title their sermons. Others don't. We think it is a helpful to the listener in concisely capturing the sermon's main thrust. Fasol states, "The title summarizes and gives direction to the sermon"[6] For instance, we might title Mark 9:33–37 as a question: "Serving Your Way to Greatness?"

---

[5] Fasol, *Essentials for Biblical Preaching*, 58.
[6] Fasol, *Essentials for Biblical Preaching*, 58.

In this case, a title presented as a question provokes thought; indeed, a thought exactly opposite of what we might expect. Stating the title early-on gives the audience some clue as to why this is important. A helpful tip: Drop-in the title at several points during the sermon. This can serve to reinforce the thrust of the message. We discovered from studying African-American preaching, specifically, that repetition can be an effective tool in driving the biblical author's intention deep into the listener's heart.

Draft Your Sermon Outline

The flow of the passage will dictate the sermon outline. Remember Walt Kaiser's two points here: (1) use present-tense phrases and (2) limit your subpoints. Too many points may convolute the text's force.

Mark 9:33-37 has a simple outline: Three main points, no sub-points. Each point marks a specific break in the biblical author's thought-flow;

I. Guard Against the Pride of Greatness (Mark 9:33-34)

II. Embrace the Principle of Greatness (Mark 9:35)

III. Imitate the Picture of Greatness (Mark 9:36-37).

Notice, each point begins with an imperative verb and is a complete sentence. Use imperatives when possible. They tend to stimulate listeners to respond. Don't force it, though. Some texts are not conducive to imperatives.

Finally, this outline happened to be alliterative. Don't try to force alliteration. Often, in trying to conjure-up alliterative words, we end up exegeting our alliteration rather than the biblical text. By Monday morning, hardly anyone will remember the alliterative points anyway.

Fill-in the Skeleton

The sermon content generally is made up of three functional elements: (1) explanation; (2) illustration; and, (3) application. A healthy sermon should use variations of each to cast light upon the biblical text. The critical idea to remember is this: in the sermon, every paragraph under a main point should connect directly to that main point. If it doesn't, then strike it.

Conclusion

To close, notice what this process does:

1. It begins with the biblical text.
2. The single meaning emerges directly from the preaching-text;

3. The timeless principle emerges directly from the single meaning;
4. The major objective of the sermon (MOS) emerges directly from the timeless principle;
5. The title emerges directly from the MOS;
6. The outline emerges directly from the MOS and takes into consideration the syntax/thought-flow of the biblical author.

In this way, every sentence in the message can be traced back to the biblical text. Indeed, every sentence will be grounded in Holy Scripture authority. We hope this little process will save you hours of wasted time in sermon preparation.

31

Drafting A Sermon Outline

You can't read 2 Timothy without coming to the conclusion the "sermon" is one of the cardinal weapons God uses to expose dark spiritual forces. Indeed, the sermon shines the light of the gospel into the kingdom of darkness. As human depravity increases at breakneck speed (2 Tim 3:1ff), Paul implores Timothy, "Preach the Word" (2 Tim 4:2). The sermon not only shines light into Satan's world system, it also lightens the path of faithful Christian saints. As such, how we organize and present our King's dictates becomes important.

When you sit down to draft a sermon outline, where do you start? What I mean is: we all start the biblical text—of course—but where do we go from there?

In thinking through the homiletical process we detailed in earlier chapters, we must keep several things in order. First, the most important element you carry over from your hermeneutics is the *"timeless principle."* Second, make certain the subject of the biblical text is the subject of your sermon. Third, retain in your sermon the emphases the biblical author preserved in the grammar of his text.

Now it's time to begin thinking through how the biblical author's thought-movements will be transferred to the sermon outline. Oftentimes, the faithful preacher does all the hard, exegetical grit-work, only to abandon it all when he sits down to prepare his sermon outline. Worse, in an effort to pacify his troubled conscience, he attributes his lack of discipline to the "movement" of the Holy Spirit!

A couple of points should help remedy this problem.

Make the Text's Main Points the Sermon's Main Points

Mirror the biblical author's emphasis in your presentation. The natural divisions of the text, by this stage, will have become clear. For instance, Let's return to Matthew 28:18-20.

Matthew writes to convince Jewish people that Jesus is the Messiah (citing over 60 OT scriptures Jesus fulfilled).[1] When Matthew comes to the end, he's still seeking to convince his readers. Matthew 28:15: "And this story has been spread among the Jews" (i.e., that the disciples

---

[1] This is the "controlling theme" of the Matthew's Gospel, a concept we discussed in an earlier chapter.

stole Jesus dead body). A clear break occurs in Matthew 28:16, "Now . . ." At this point, let's move from hermeneutics into homiletics.

First, our hermeneutical study yielded a *timeless principle* which sounds something like this: *Jesus's authority grounds us in who we are, what we do, and with Whom we serve.*

Second, Matthew constructed the paragraph in such a way that the "authority" of Jesus (v. 18) accomplishes three things: (1) it relieves our "doubt" (vv. 16-17); (2) it authenticates our mission (vv. 19-20a); and, (3) it comforts as we go (v. 20b). Verses 16-17 flow into Christ's "authority" (v. 18). Verses 19-20 flow out of it. Now, we see the main points beginning to take shape:

I. His Authority Relieves Your Doubts (28:16-18)

II. His Authority Empowers Your Mission (28:19-20a)

   A. Make Disciples

      1. By going

      2. By baptizing

      3. By teaching

III. His Authority Overpowers Opposition (28:20b).

Or, if we wanted to prompt our listeners to action (as Matthew desires), then use imperatives (discussed below). Jesus's authority empowers His saints to:

I. Trust Him Completely (28:16-18)

II. Disciple Others Energetically (28:19-20a)

    A. By going

    B. By baptizing

    C. By teaching

III. Press on Confidently (28:20b).

The "meat" of the passage comes in verses 19-20a. It contains the strongest verb, "make disciples;" and therefore, should be given the place of primacy in the sermon. Make sure your presentation mirrors that emphasis. Timewise, spend more time developing point II than the others. Matthew concentrates his emphasis on verses 19-20a. Follow his lead.

The beauty is this: other "authorities" may attempt to hinder us. Secular authorities may attempt to silence us; family authorities may attempt to pressure us; societal authorities may attempt to marginalize us. No matter. We have divine authority which transcends all of those. This is precisely the reason Jesus adds Matthew 28:20b: To encourage us because His divine message will encounter opposition.

Use Present-Tense Verbs in Your Outline

Walt Kaiser offers a practical, but often unnoticed, point of wisdom: Use strong, present-tense verbs in your outline.[2]

If God's Word is timeless (and it is), then we should speak in present-tense terms. As Kaiser notes, presenting Numbers 22:1-35 in the following (past-tense) format loses some of its present-day impact:

I. Balaam Sought (Numbers 22:1-20)

II. Balaam Fought (Numbers 22:21-27)

III. Balaam Taught (Numbers 22:28-38).

A better outline would be this: "Knowing & Doing the Will of God:"

I. By Keeping the Faith (Numbers 22:1-7)

II. By Obeying God's Word (Numbers 22:8-22)

III. By Observing the Obstacles (Numbers 22:23-35).

Imperatives often sharpen the focus even more:

I. Keep the Faith (Numbers 22:1-7)

II. Obey the Word (Numbers 22:8-22)

---

[2] Kaiser, *Toward an Exegetical Theology*, 157-59.

III. Observe the Obstacles (Numbers 22:23–35)

Simply using present-tense verbs brings the audience from ancient times into the here-and-now relevance (note also: the verse divisions changed to more accurately reflect the biblical author's text divisions). It helps if the outline is consistent grammatically. That is, if one point is a phrase, all should be a phrase; if one point is a single word, all should be a single word; if one point is a sentence, all should be a sentence. This is not always possible, but it will help the listener when it is possible.

Closing Thought

Try these two exercises for a month. Your listeners will comment on how your preaching or teaching is different (in a positive way). They won't be able to put their finger on why, but you will.

32

Thinking Through the Entire Sermon

Suppose you are called upon to preach 1 John 3:1-10. By this point, you've already done all the hermeneutical and some homiletical work. Now, it is time to start thinking through how this preaching-text drives the shape and content of your sermon so you can present it in a clear and cogent way. Your thoughts must take into account both (1) your hermeneutical conclusions and (2) your homiletical conclusions.

Hermeneutical Conclusions

Concisely summarize your hermeneutical conclusions by asking the following questions.

1. What does the canonical analysis tell us? 1 John is one of the last letters written in the NT. Also, the author wrote the Gospel of John prior to writing 1 John.

2. What does the book analysis tell us?

    a. Who is the author? Authorship generally is attributed to John, the fisherman and apostle. He also wrote the Gospel of John, 2 John, 3 John, and Revelation.

    b. Who is the audience? We don't know with certainty. He writes to believers (1 Jn 5:13). We know they were dealing with apostasy (1 Jn 2:19) and false teachers (1 Jn 2:22).

    c. When was it written? Most scholars date it late first century.

    d. Are there any unique syntactical markings? Scholars have suggested John provides three tests by which professing Christians can assess whether or not they (or others) truly are Christians. These tests would be a welcomed relief to those facing apostasy of loved ones and false teaching in the early congregations. The three tests are meant to cause assurance (not doubt) of salvation:

        i. A doctrinal test. Do I believe in the correct Jesus correctly?

        ii. A moral test. Do I have a correct behavior regarding obedience?

Thinking Through the Entire Sermon

       iii. A social test. Do I have a correct attitude toward others?[1]

       John cycles through these tests, somewhat randomly, throughout his letter. This fits John's style as he seems to think topically rather than chronologically, even in his Gospel. Therefore, the first task is to determine which test John is applying in our preaching-text.

   e. What is the letter's single purpose? John's states his purpose is in 1 John 5:13: "I write these things to you who believe in the name of the Son of God that you may know that you have eternal life." Again, members of this congregation were apostatizing (1 Jn 2:19). John, therefore, issues three tests by which a person can judge whether he/she (or those apostatizing) is a true child of God.

3. What does the sectional context tell us? In chapter 1, John lays out his three tests. In chapters 2 and 3, he gets more specific. He contrasts those who do not live righteously with those who do. He does

---

[1] See James Montgomery Boice, *The Epistles of John* (Grand Rapids: Baker Books, 1979, paperback, 2006), 14; D. A. Carson, Douglas Moo, and Leon Morris, *An Introduction to the New Testament* (Grand Rapids: Zondervan, 1992), 445; Thomas D. Lea, *The New Testament: Its Background and Message* (Nashville, TN: Broadman & Holman, 1996), 564.

this with a mantra of "we do this . . . they do that" distinctions to sharpen his point.

4. What does the immediate context tell us? The immediate context focuses on the moral test (obedience).

Homiletical Conclusions

At this point, take all of your hermeneutical considerations and create your steps to the sermon as follows:

Single Meaning: John drew clear distinctions between God's children and the devil's children.

Timeless Principle: Those who are genuine Christians will be "obvious."

Major Objective of the Sermon (MOS): To stimulate believers to live "obvious" Christian lives.

Sermon Title: "No Fruit, No Root"

Outline:

Introduction
John Bunyan wrote a book about the funeral of a non-Christian: *The Life & Death of Mr. Badman*. It recounts the story of a sinner who went to hell. The point is: Genuine

Thinking Through the Entire Sermon

Christians will live a life characterized by Christ-likeness; not perfection, but progressively becoming more Christ-like. In other words, "No fruit, no root."

I. *We* Purify Ourselves (3:1–3).

II. *They* Live a Lifestyle of Sin (3:4–5).

III. *We* Live a Lifestyle of Righteousness (3:6–7).

IV. *They* are Children of The Devil (3:8).

V. *We* are Children of God (3:9).

VI. Genuine Believers will be Obvious (Evident) (3:10).

Closing

Is it evident ("obvious") in my life? The same tests that are meant as assurances to true believers can torment the consciences of false converts or cultural Christians. Take time to examine yourself.

Closing Thoughts

This passage is unusual in that there are six thought-units (represented by six points). Obviously, be judicious with the time you allot to each point (something we discuss in a later chapter). Make clear from the start that (1) John wrote to believers and (2) he wasn't preaching a works-based righteousness. John's point is clear: A righteous lifestyle is not a means of saving grace; rather, it is the visible fruit of saving grace. The fruit of true believers will be evident to the watching world.

This exercise will seem tedious at first, but it will yield terrific results. It keeps us tethered to the author's single-meaning. Sermons grounded in such biblical authority have the power to change men's hearts. Sermons that stray become weak and powerless. We want the former, not the latter.

33

Should I Have Heretics in My Home?

Have you ever met a false teacher? Most likely you have but didn't know it. They don't walk around with pitchforks and horns growing out of their heads. No, they are charming, winsome, and speak silky smooth words. They often come bearing gifts, enjoying your company, and even doing kind deeds. Yet, their real work is undercover. Their end-game is to sink their roots deep into the heart of unsuspecting souls. They masquerade as servants of righteousness (2 Cor. 11:15), but behind their Dr. Jekyll façade rages a Mr. Hyde in all his wickedness. Much of the NT is concerned with the corruptive efforts of false teachers. 2 John, specifically, shares that concern.

My first significant interaction with 2 John occurred when I visited a small group in Texas. Oh, I'd read it many times—it being a short letter—but I'd never studied it seriously. The small group quickly came to a point of disagreement.

John advocates: If anyone comes to you who is not teaching the correct Christ correctly, then "do not receive him into your house." Two people in the class voiced opposing opinions: (1) one felt that this command no longer applies today because it would be rude behavior (especially to someone who needs the gospel); (2) the other person felt it did apply today, and that we should forbid having people in our homes who might disagree with us on spiritual matters. Which one is correct?

Let us apply our hermeneutical and homiletical principles, and see where it leads.

Hermeneutical Considerations

1. What does the canonical analysis tell us? This is one of the last letters written in the NT. Before this, the author wrote the Gospel of John and 1 John, which we can consult if necessary.

2. What does the book analysis tell us?

    a. Who is the author? Most scholars accept John as author, the fisherman and apostle of Jesus Christ.

    b. Who is the audience? We don't know the audience with certainty. It is addressed to the "elect lady." However, much of the letter addresses the "elect lady" in the 2nd person plural. Therefore, it seems likely he is writing to a congregation. Or, perhaps, he was writing to the lady in whose home the congregation met.

c. When was it written? Most scholars date it late first century.

d. Are there any unique syntactical markings? 1 John 3:1-4 is a typical greeting, and then the letter neatly breaks into 3 parts: (1) God's request (vv. 5-6); (2) God's warning (vv. 7-9); and, (3) God's wisdom (vv. 10-11). John closes with a somewhat urgent salutation in verses 12-13.

e. What is the author's single purpose? John doesn't state his purpose precisely, as he does in his Gospel or in 1 John. However, his clear emphasis is a stern warning concerning false teachers. Simply put: John warned against being hoodwinked by false teachers.

3. What does the sectional context tell us? This entire letter is only 245 words. It's short enough for one sermon (although it could be broken into smaller units). Two ideas are prominent: (1) keep loving one another and (2) do not be duped by false teachers. Those two ideas really converge into one: One way you love one another is to protect one another

from false teachers. John appears to be saying that—if they band together in Christian love—it will be difficult for false teachers to penetrate their congregation.

4. What does the immediate context tell us? John aims to unify the congregation to combat deceptive teachers. A study of first century hospitality helps clarify the context. Hospitality was expected in general. Christians, specifically, showed Christ's love by being extra hospitable, even housing guests for long periods of time. In John's day, a true dilemma arose. Christians were expected to show overly generous hospitality, but false teachers were quick to hold them hostage to that. MacArthur even suggests they were setting up headquarters in the homes of members and guilting them into longer stays.[1] Remember, they had no church buildings in those days. They met in homes. The false teachers may have been staying in the home in which the church met, which would add another layer of complexity to the situation.

---

[1] MacArthur states that false teachers were "taking advantage of Christian hospitality to advance their cause (vv. 10–11; cf. Rom. 12:13; Heb. 13:2; 1 Pet. 4:9)." See MacArthur, *The John MacArthur Study Bible*, 1975.

Should I Have Heretics in My Home?

Homiletical Considerations

Single Meaning: John encouraged the saints to love one another by protecting against false teachers.

Timeless Principle: Love fellow believers by exposing false teachers.

Major Objective of the Sermon (MOS): To highlight how protecting the saints from false teachers is a loving act.

Sermon Title: "Should I Have a Heretic in My House?

Outline:

Introduction

True love has a dimension often ignored. It can be uncomfortable and confrontational. We call it "tough love." An example: I spoke to a parent whose child was homeless, destitute, and down-and-out. This had happened before, many times. It always led to the same place. Parental help, even with good intentions, enabled the child's degeneration. This situation called for "tough love." Another, even more heart-wrenching, example: I spoke with a person who had to take away the car keys of their aging parent. It was becoming dangerous to the parent and the public. This is "tough love." Love is a servant, but not a doormat.

Love has a gentle side, but love has a firm side, too. John speaks to the firm side here.

I. Background Setting (vv. 1-4)

II. God's Request: Love One Another (vv. 5-6)

III. God's Warning: Watch for False Teachers (vv. 7-9)

IV. God's Wisdom: Do Not Aid or Abet False Teachers (vv. 10-11)

V. Salutation (vv. 12-13).

Closing
Illustration: Think of an example of the far-reaching impact of corruptive false teaching.

Closing Thoughts

The first century context of hospitality gives direction to the specific application. Within your points, align your time in concert with John's emphasis. Use the first point to set the first century context of hospitality. Practically speaking, I would aim for the following allocations: Point 1 (2-3 min.), Point 2 (2-3 min.), Point 3 (10 min.), Point 4 (10 min.), Point 5 (1 min.).

The justification for these time allocations is not always the "number" of verses, but rather the "thrust" of the verses. Clearly, John roots the issue in self-sacrificial love, but his "thrust" is to address the false teachers. More exegetical work is required in Point 3 (theology of "Christ in the flesh," defining "antichrist," etc.) and Point 4 (exegeting the term, *greeting* and making present-day application).

Back to the small group I mentioned. Which position was correct? Our exegesis reveals a couple of important items:

1. John is not speaking of teachers who may be "confused" on certain doctrinal matters. Rather, he is speaking about those who bring a clear set of false teachings. They have wicked motives. Oftener than not, the motive is to accumulate status or riches for themselves. Beware of those people. Yet, we must distinguish between those who might be "confused" on Christ's teachings (i.e., Apollos, Acts 18:26) from those who are wickedly opposed to them or undermining them. Sometimes in the NT, Paul removed false teachers from the church. Other times, he advised to patiently endure, correcting them with gentleness (2 Tim 4:2). We must make careful and discerning distinctions.

2. Are we never to allow someone into our home who might disagree with us on doctrine? I don't believe so. That application does not align with the first

century term, "*greeting,*" as John used it. Otherwise, you could not allow the pagan plumber in to fix your busted pipe! However, if we truly love other believers, we must exercise extreme caution not to endorse, aid, abet, or encourage people whose motivation is to lead others away from Christ. Remember, God makes no call here to be rude, disrespectful, or uncivil anyone. Rather, "*greeting*" them (in John's day) would be to endorse them, offer them financial support, or do anything to advance their cause.

34

Power Struggles in the Congregation

Have you ever experienced power struggles in your congregation? I received a call one day. My pastor-friend was distraught. He had received a written letter from a female staff member. She accused him of sexual harassment. The letter demanded he resign immediately. Otherwise, she would tell the congregation. It was an hour's drive, but I went straight there to be with him.

Once I arrived and collected the facts, I told him, "Frame the letter. It will be the visible reminder of reformation in this congregation." The truth was, he never touched her or harassed her in any way. He contacted an attorney and demanded a written retraction. She admitted she had lied. She offered a full retraction and immediately resigned. When the dust settled, that situation revealed a deeper issue: a power struggle within the congregation, and she was at the center of it.

Third John provides practical wisdom on how to deal with power struggles in the congregation. Let's assume you have completed an exegetical study of the letter. Now, let's work through your hermeneutical and homiletical conclusions.

Hermeneutical Conclusions

1. What does the canonical analysis tell us? This is one of the last letters written in the NT. Before this, John also wrote the Gospel of John, 1 John, and 2 John. We can consult John's prior writings if we run into difficulties on a particular issue.
2. What does the book analysis tell us?
   a. Who is the author? Most scholars consider the Apostle John is the author.
   b. Who is the audience? The recipient is Gaius. We know nothing of him for certain, other than he was a faithful Christian "walking in the truth" (v. 3). Likely, he was a convert of the Apostle John (v. 4).
   c. When was it written? Most scholars date it in the late first century.
   d. Are there any unique syntactical markings? After a short greeting (v. 1), John builds his letter around four personalities:[1]

---

[1] See Daniel Akin, *1, 2, 3 John*, vol. 38, NAC (Nashville: B&H, 2001), 237–38.

Power Struggles in the Congregation

      i. Gaius: Strive to Set a Christly Example (vv. 2-8)

     ii. Diotrephes: Stop Divisive Behavior (vv. 9-10)

    iii. Demetrius: Build a Godly Testimony (vv. 11-12)

    iv. John: Show Genuine Care (vv. 13-15).

e. What is the author's purpose? John doesn't state his purpose outright. However, the letter's structure makes his purpose clear: To address a power struggle disrupting the congregation. He contrasts the godliness of Gaius and Demetrius against the ungodliness of the main culprit, Diotrephes. Simply put: *John gave biblical instruction on how to address power struggles in the congregation.*

f. What is the sectional context? A division in the congregation centered around one person: Diotrephes. Therefore, John gave counsel on how to confront this troublemaker.

g. What is the immediate context? John heard this agitator was causing problems (even preventing growth, v. 10). He calls them to faithfully follow Christ in love by addressing a divisive personality.

Homiletical Conclusions

Single Meaning: John gave biblical directives on how to address power struggles plaguing the congregation.

Timeless Principle: Combat division in the congregation by faithfully applying Christ's truth-principles.

Major Objective: Focus on overcoming evil by doing the right things for the right reason in the right spirit.

Sermon Title: "Power Struggles in the Congregation"

Outline:

I. Strive To Set a Christly Example (Gaius) (vv. 2–8)
II. Stop Divisive Behavior (Diotrophes) (vv. 9–10)
III. Build A Godly Testimony (Demetrius) (vv. 11–12)
IV. Show Genuine Care (John) (vv. 13–15)

Closing Thoughts

This sermon sets up nicely for strong, imperative outline points. Such imperatives offer the listener practical biblical truths to apply to his/her life. Of course, you can

Power Struggles in the Congregation

split the letter into smaller preaching-units, but it also is short enough to preach as a single unit.

The emphasis of the letter is on stopping the rabble-rouser, Diotrophes. Settle in on Point II in the sermon. Track his actions as detailed in the biblical text. Most power mongers unconsciously follow the same pattern. Here is how you will recognize a present-day Diotrophes (or Jezebel):

- *Pride*: "he [or she] puts himself [or herself] first" (v. 9). It is rumored C.S. Lewis once said, "Pride is the mother hen under which all other sins are hatched."[2] Power struggles always begin with pride. From human pride springs forth all manner of other divisive sins: greed, gossip, slander, covetousness, rebellion, idolatry, etc.

- *Rejection of authority*: "does not acknowledge authority" (v. 9). A divisive person will rebel against authority: God's authority, Scriptural authority, or

---

[2] Though this quote is attributed to C. S. Lewis, I have not been able to verify it. Brad Mitchell attributes it to C.S. Lewis in Lee Strobel's, *A Case for Grace* (Grand Rapids: Zondervan, 2015), 128.

Whether Lewis penned it or not, it accurately reflects Lewis's view. Lewis said, "According to Christian teachers, the essential vice, the utmost evil, is Pride. Unchastity, anger, greed, drunkenness, and all that, are mere fleabites in comparison: it was through Pride that the devil become the devil: Pride leads to every other vice: it is the complete anti-God state of mind." See C. S. Lewis, *Mere Christianity*, Book 3, chapter 8, "The Great Sin," accessible online here: https://dacc.edu/assets/pdfs/PCM/merechristianitylewis.pdf.

pastoral authority. It doesn't matter to him or her. He or she will seek to establish himself/herself as the greater authority.

- *Gossip*: "talking wicked nonsense" (v. 10). This person will engage in private conversations, lurking from house to house, saying things in private they would not say in public; or nowadays, weaponizing social media for disingenuous purposes. They never call names outright. They are too cowardly for that. Rather, they speak in terms general enough that they can't be indicted but specific enough that everyone knows who they are targeting: typically the Lead Pastor. God sees all these iniquitous deeds, and He never forgets.
- *Group control*: "refuses to welcome the brothers, and also stops those who want to" (v. 10). The last stage will be to build-up a coalition. They will prey upon a group of vulnerable people, convincing them to join rank through soothing words, half lies, bribes, and tall tales. If you disagree with the "group think," they will alienate or shun you. Don't get caught up in such power struggle politics. Stay above the fray.

In light of this, the question looms, "How do you deal with such venomous vipers?" First, expound Holy Scripture: This is the "truth" God mentions five times in this letter. The preaching of Holy Scripture will accomplish two things: (1) it will expose their wicked deeds and (2) it will embolden mature Christians to purge out devilish activities which are corrupting Christ's Bride.

Second, "bring up what he [or she] is doing" (v. 10). God grants us permission and authority in this letter to expose those who are dividing the congregation. We have permission to call names, to present any false (or misleading) statements made, and to cast light on evil behavior. Notice, though, John didn't excommunicate the malcontent from the congregation. He had the authority to do so, but (in this instance) he refrained. On the other hand, Paul did excommunicate malcontents on occasion (1 Tim 1:20). Remain cautious, careful, patient, and allow God time to act before you do. At the same time, don't keep things hidden: "bring up" the things causing division. The time may come to confront and discipline, but be extremely careful in the meanwhile. While you wait, encourage the members (as John did) to support the direction of the congregation (as long as it is scriptural) and keep confronting those who won't.

Ultimately, you may need to exercise congregational discipline in accord with Matthew 18:15–20. This is not always easy to accomplish because these slithering vipers are cunning, clever, and almost always cover their tracks. It may be difficult to prove their sin against you. What's worse, you may be outnumbered in the short-term. Be patient. Keep preaching. Keep shining light on the wicked deeds. At some point, the tyrant will expose himself, and the truth will come out. In the meanwhile, handle yourself with the grace of Demetrius: Keep doing the right thing for the right reason in the right spirit. Just as Jannes and Jambres opposed Moses, the folly of these evildoers will be plain to all (2 Tim 3:8–9).

Above all, stand strong and represent our King well.

35

How Many Minutes Should a Sermon Last?

How many times have you heard, jokingly, "Well, if the preacher hadn't been so longwinded, . . .?"

I tell people, "Time goes by so fast when you're standing in the pulpit and so slow when you're sitting in the pew!" Believe me, I know. I've been on both sides! It raises the question, though: How many minutes should your sermon last?

Sermons in Scripture

Actual sermons in Scripture run both ends of the spectrum. Perhaps the greatest sermon ever preached, the Sermon on the Mount, was less than twelve minutes long (Matt 5-7). Peter's sermon at Pentecost was less than three minutes long, and 3,000 souls were saved (Acts 2). If Hebrews is a sermon, as some suggest, it would have lasted about forty-five minutes.

On the other hand, Paul once "prolonged his speech until midnight" in Troas (Acts 20:7). One young man fell asleep in a windowsill and fell three stories to his apparent death, Eutychus. One preacher said, "You'd-a-cussed (Eu-ty-chus), too, if Paul preached that long!"

The point is this: sermons in Scripture vary in length. What's more, it seems they took their audience and setting into account. We probably should, too. After all, no one in their right mind (we hope) would preach a three-hour Puritan-style sermon to preschoolers.

Is the Strength in the Length?

John Calvin didn't think so. Commenting on 1 Corinthians 14:29, where Paul limits (to three) the number of prophets allowed to speak, Calvin states, "Paul considered what the weakness of men could bear."[1] Calvin's own sermons, when read aloud, typically range anywhere from eight minutes to sixty minutes. Or, as my deacon (a retired school teacher) wisely warned, "'The mind can bear no more than the rear end can endure!'"

This is not to suggest longer sermons are less effective or that shorter sermons are preferred. It is only to observe this: sermon length in Scripture and throughout church

---

[1] John Calvin, *Commentary on the Epistles of Paul the Apostle to the Corinthians*, vol. 1, trans. by John Pringle (Grand Rapids: Baker Books, reprinted 2005), 460.

history varied. Therefore, we cannot say the "strength is in the length."

Neil Postman wrote a fascinating little volume entitled, *Amusing Ourselves to Death*.[2] It's a book about the modern man's diminishing attention span. We are bombarded with thousands of pieces of information daily: billboards, advertisements, street signs, radio ads, etc. Open your computer and ads pop up every five seconds. Television scenes change angles every two or three seconds. We tap our phones, at times, more than once per second. All of this trains the brain to jump constantly.

It has had an effect. People today have trouble looking you in the eye, much less enduring a ninety-minute sermon. They are accustomed to a blitzkrieg of information bombarding them from all angles. As technology has advanced, attention spans have decreased. Postman's thesis, essentially, was this: The only remedy to shortened attention spans is more lecture-styled exposition.

We sympathize with Postman's point. At the same time, we wonder—with the sermon in particular—if this should be a wholescale, immediate change or more of a gradual turning of the ship. After all, most of society—even those faithful congregation members—have been reared on sound-bytes, sports highlights, and cheeky tweets. No one watches a nine-inning baseball game

---

[2] Neil Postman, *Amusing Ourselves to Death* (New York, NY: Penguin Group, 1986).

anymore when we can pull up the highlights on our cell phone. A two to three-hour Puritanesque sermon may be asking too much from today's audience. Jesus certainly didn't demand that of His listeners on the mount (Matt 5-7) or at the beach (Matt 13). Yet, Paul went long (albeit, to an entirely different audience), and poor Eutychus simply could not endure (Acts 20:9). I somewhat sympathize with Eutychus myself!

We wonder how helpful it is when others browbeat listeners for their inability to endure hour long messages. Perhaps we should recognize: (1) most of us are not gifted orators like Spurgeon; (2) our inefficient use of time chasing rabbits in the pulpit is not the listener's fault; and (3) our listeners' brains can take only so much divine truth in one sitting.

God revealed all truth progressively, not all in one sitting. Preachers often reveal all truth in one sitting, not progressively. We wonder why.

Closing Thoughts

One of my favorite preachers on earth is in a small town in Alabama. Few have heard his name: Tom Hannah. His messages, typically, are about twenty minutes (sometimes less), but they are packed with powerful, poignant, passionate gospel truth. Another of my favorite preachers is in California. Many *have* heard his name, John

MacArthur. His messages, typically, are about sixty minutes, but they, too, are packed with powerful, poignant, passionate gospel truth. Both have recognized their giftedness, and both exercise it appropriately.

What, exactly, are we suggesting? We are suggesting there can be strength in length, *and* we are suggesting brevity can be beneficial. Yet, is the number of minutes the primary concern?

We think not, and we will suggest why in the next chapter.

36

Sermon Length and the Sufficiency of Scripture

A friend and I were discussing the appropriate length of a sermon from one of Paul's letters. "Which rabbits are you chasing?" my friend asked rhetorically, "Are you chasing Paul's rabbits or your own?" Often, our sermons are too long because we're chasing the wrong rabbits.

As mentioned in the last chapter, actual sermons in Scripture (and in church history) vary in length. Rather than quibble over whether to preach sixty-minutes vs. twelve-minutes, we are interested in a more pertinent issue: The minutes you allot to each point within the sermon (no matter the sermon's length). We feel the implications of those "minute-allotments" have a direct bearing on the doctrine of the sufficiency of Scripture. No preaching book I know of makes this connection. We wonder why.

To truly uphold the sufficiency of Scripture, you must "weight" your points in alignment with the biblical author's emphases (see prior chapters). Ultimately, this comes down to assigning a specified number of minutes to each point, sub-point, sub-sub-point, etc. To allot more minutes to a minor point and less minutes to a major point "could" misconstrue the biblical author's intent. Who grants us the authority to take such liberties? If God has spoken in Scripture—and He has—isn't it only fair (and right) that we honor His "breathed-out" emphases in our presentation to men?

For instance, our sermon may have three points, but the biblical author might emphasize the last point more than the others. The last point demands more minutes within the sermon than the other two. Otherwise, we implicitly deny the sufficiency of Scripture by over (or under) emphasizing points more (or less) than did the biblical author.

Again, imagine someone stood to explain a short letter you wrote about an urgent issue. In their thirty-minute explanation, suppose they spent two minutes on the urgent issue and twenty-eight minutes expounding your three-word salutation? How would you feel about that? In principle, it's no different than Joel Osteen accentuating the positive portions of a preaching-text and minimizing (or ignoring altogether) the negative injunctions. It denies the sufficiency of Scripture in the delivery.

A Biblical Example

Recently, we heard a pastor preach from Ephesians 4:7-16. That paragraph speaks of congregation members using their gifts in cooperation (not competition). Within that paragraph, the Apostle Paul added a parenthetical statement (4:9-10). He states Jesus "descended into the lower regions, the earth?" Commentaries tend to allot more pages to that mysterious phrase than to the Apostle's larger point. That is, did Jesus descend into Hades to proclaim victory over wicked spirits in prison (Tertullian, Jerome); or, did He descend to Sheol to rescue those held captive by the devil before Christ's first coming (Aquinas); or, did he descend to paradise in Sheol to release the OT saints into heaven (MacArthur); or, did He descend to earth in His incarnation (which included the grave) (Calvin)? This is a knotty issue that quickly can gobble up valuable minutes of sermon time. We wondered how the preacher would navigate those waters.

We felt he handled it well. He let the listener know that this two-verse parenthetical has been debated for centuries. He quickly shared the differing views throughout the history of interpretation. He stated which view he preferred and why. Then, he pivoted to show us how that parenthetical advanced Paul's larger point: Christ secured the gifts; distributed them to His elect children as He saw fit; and therefore, we are to use our gifts in cooperation with one another, not competition. In a forty-minute sermon, he devoted about five minutes to that parenthetical. We felt he made an honest attempt to honor the great doctrine of the sufficiency of Scripture in his delivery.

Closing Thoughts

First, we suggest one last step in your sermon preparation: Assign "minute-allotments" to each point within your sermon based on the author's intended emphases. Try to stay within those allotments in your delivery. Your listeners will appreciate this. More importantly, your delivery will serve to honor the foundational doctrine of the sufficiency of Scripture.

Second, think through the entire length of your sermon in terms of total minutes. How many minutes should a sermon be? That depends on context. We served in a seminary town for several years. The congregation there was accustomed to forty-five-plus minute sermons. We also have served in a more blue-collar setting. Practically (unless you're an extremely gifted orator), if you don't get your point across in 20-25 minutes, you're edifying only yourself. This is not to suggest those minutes cannot be expanded over time. For instance, we've also served in a place where members were accustomed to 15-20 minute sermons. Gradually, over the years, their listening capacity was expanded to 40-45 minutes without losing anyone

Sermon Length and the Sufficiency of Scripture

along the way. Again, we stress, our stated goal is not to increase the audience's listening capacity. Our goal is to convey accurately the biblical author's intent: whether it takes you ten minutes or two hours.

Third, vary the length of your sermons, depending on the passage. This accomplishes two things: (1) it keeps your listeners from settling into a "routine," which can hinder the freshness of worship and (2) it forces you to be efficient with your words and delivery. We all tend to have an exalted view of our oratorical abilities, but strength is not always in the length. Sometimes, brevity is better. Yet, honoring the sufficiency of Scripture in our delivery is best of all.

37

Chasing the Wrong Rabbits

Sometimes, the superiority of expository sermons is seen best in light of a non-expository sermon. Let me share one for comparison purposes.[1] The preaching-text was Luke 5:1–11. Before analyzing the sermon, let's familiarize ourselves with Luke's intent.

Luke's Intent

The clear meaning, based on an exegetical study, is this: *Luke took deliberate aim to convince his readers that Jesus is God in the flesh.*[2] Let's document this from Luke's text. This preaching-text falls within a section spotlighting Jesus' divine authority and nature:

---

[1] The sermon is the Presidential Address preached by Bobby Welch at the 2005 Southern Baptist Convention Pastor's Conference, titled, "Deep Water Doers."

[2] This truth-claim will be supported by other theological scholarship below.

1. In Luke 4:31-37, Jesus healed a demon-possessed man. The demon referred to Him as "the Holy One of God" (4:34) and the people were amazed at Jesus' "authority" (4:36).

2. In Luke 4:38-40, Jesus healed many. The demons cried out, "You are the Son of God"—a reference to Jesus's divinity.

3. In Luke 4:43, Luke recorded Jesus's claim that He was sent from heaven to announce the coming of the Kingdom of God.

4. In our preaching text, Jesus performed an extraordinary miracle in which the disciples caught a tremendous haul of fish during non-peak hours.

5. In Luke 5:12-16, Luke recorded Jesus healing a leper.

6. In Luke 5:17-26, Jesus dramatically healed a paralytic. He equated Himself with God, declaring He possessed authority to forgive sins (5:22-25).

7. In 5:33-35, Luke documented Jesus's claim to be the bridegroom, a reference to Himself as Head of God's people (5:33-35).

8. Finally, in Luke 6:1-5, Jesus named Himself as Lord of the Sabbath, something only God could do.

Clearly, Luke was building a case. When we return to 5:1-11, the obvious point becomes clear. Luke used this event to establish a fine point: To be in Jesus's presence is to be in God's presence. Peter recognized this, and fell at His feet in an act of repentant worship.

Confirmation of Luke's Intent

I checked myself with others. They confirm the same. For instance,

> MacArthur: "Peter immediately recognized he was in the presence of the Holy One exercising His divine power, and he was stricken with shame over his own sin."[3]

> Calvin: "The design of the miracle undoubtedly was, to make known Christ's divinity, and thus induce Peter and others to become his disciples."[4]

Robert Stein, Darrell Bock, I. Howard Marshall and others confirm the same.[5] At this point, we feel confident in

---

[3] *John MacArthur Study Bible*, 1521 (notes on Luke 5:8).
[4] John Calvin, *Commentary on a Harmony of the Evangelists, Matthew, Mark, and Luke*, vol. 1 (Grand Rapids: Baker Books, reprint, 2005), 241.
[5] See Robert H. Stein, *Luke*, New American Commentaries, vol. 24 (Nashville: Broadman, 1992); Darrell Bock, *Luke: 1:1–9:50* (BECNT, vol. 1 (Grand Rapids: Baker, 1994), 452; I. Howard Marshall, *The Gospel of Luke*, NIGCT (Grand Rapids: Eerdmans, 1978), 199-200.

saying: Luke sought to convince his readers that Jesus is God in the flesh.

A Non-Expository Sermon

What if I suggested to you that Luke's intent was something different entirely? Welch declares, rather forcefully, "Jesus is about to unfold a personalized, simplified, systematic, theology for soul-winning. . . . It's not very hard to get it, and he made it overwhelming clear in this passage."[6] Is that what Luke intended to convey?

What if I told you this little pericope taught the "shore" represents the "church;" the "deep waters" represent the world; letting down the "nets" represents faith; the "nets" themselves represent the gospel; and, the "fish" represent lost souls?

Further, what if I proclaimed with authority that all this indicates Jesus was unfolding a personalized, simplified, systematic theology for soul-winning? The application of the text, then, becomes this: You must exercise faith to get out of the church and into the world. You must share the gospel. You must reap the harvest. And, if you do these things, then your church likely will overflow because so many converted sinners will be pouring in.

---

[6] Bobby Welch, "Deep Water Doers" (Presidential Address, Southern Baptist Convention, 2005).

Again, we ask, "Is this what Luke intended to say? Is that what God intended to communicate through him?"

Chasing the Wrong Rabbit

One of the things that affected Welch's interpretation is this: It was preached in 2005. He was the president of one of the world's largest denominations. In 2005, there was a push to "win and baptize" 1,000,000 souls. Therefore, he came to preaching text with an agenda, and he imposed that agenda onto the text. Let's pinpoint where things went wrong.

1. He ignored the book context and the sectional context. Both were establishing the divinity of Christ (not a method of evangelism).

2. He denied the "God-breathed" syntactical structures: i.e., Christ performs a miracle that authenticates his divine authority (5:1-7). Next, Peter is astonished, falling at Christ's feet in worship (5:8-10). Lastly, Luke states the design of the miracle: "[T]hey forsook all and followed him." The syntactical structures point to Christ's Lordship over all things. Nowhere does Luke suggest—much less, state—that "shore = church," "deep = world," or "nets = faith," etc.

3. This method implicitly assumes God's single, verbal meaning is not sufficient.

4. This method implicitly permits the cultural context to dictate God's meaning. The exact opposite should be the case. God's meaning should affect the culture. The culture never should affect God's meaning (even if well-intended).

5. Because Luke's intent was altered, the application was altered. The sermon centered on man (personal evangelism) rather than Christ (His authority and divinity).

Concluding Thoughts

To be clear, we have no problem with the truth the preacher proclaimed. The problem we have is he proclaimed it from the wrong text. God has supplied us with plenty of NT passages which center on the importance of personal evangelism. Why not choose one of those? By not doing so, the sufficiency of Scripture is called into question; and worse, we have modeled a method that those who follow us will take beyond what we ever dreamed. History bears out this assertion.

Here again, we must keep on asking, "Which rabbits are we chasing: Luke's rabbits or our own?" If we refuse to restrict ourselves to the verbal meaning God has revealed, then the Bible becomes malleable to our own pursuits and passions. May it never be! Scripture is God-breathed. The meaning God placed in Scripture-texts is unchangeable, immutable, and sufficient. We cannot improve upon it, so why try?

38

Preaching with Spirit-Power

John Bunyan was an uneducated tinker (metal worker) who became a preacher in England. John Owen was a great theologian, scholar, and statesman who loved to hear him preach. Why? Historian, Joseph Ivimey describes it as follows:

> Among [Bunyan's] auditors was his friend and admirer, Dr. John Owen. Charles II. it is reported, once asked the Doctor how he who had so much learning could hear a tinker preach? To which the Doctor replied, "May it please your majesty, had I the tinker's abilities for preaching, I would gladly relinquish all my learning."[1]

---

[1] Joseph Ivimey, *History of the English Baptists*, vol. 4 (London: Lutton and Son, Baynes, Gale, Curtis, and Fenner, Paternoster Row; Williams, Stationers' Court; Otridge and Bagster Strand; and Gardiner, Princes Street, Cavendish Square, 1814), 41. The full book is accessible online: https://archive.org/details/historyofenglish02ivim/page/n7/mode/2up.

We can possess all the learning in the world; we can prepare the best expository sermons on paper; but apart from the power of the Holy Spirit of God, our preaching will be impotent.

The Apostle Paul acknowledges as much in 1 Corinthians 2:1-5:

> And I, when I came to you, brothers, did not come proclaiming to you the testimony of God with lofty speech or wisdom. For I decided to know nothing among you except Jesus Christ and Him crucified. And I was with you in weakness and in fear and much trembling, and my speech and my message were not in plausible words of wisdom, but in demonstration of the Spirit and of power, so that your faith might not rest in the wisdom of men but in the power of God.

Holy Spirit Power

The "power" Paul speaks of doesn't come from how loud you yell, how must gusto you generate, or even how well you prepare. The "power" he speaks of reaches deep into your listener's hearts, awakens them to their sinful condition, causes them to cry out in faith and repentance, and transforms their attitudes, actions, and behavior. Mere words—no matter how inspirational—cannot accomplish that. We need the Word and the Spirit coupled together to plant roots deep in the ground of our listener's heart. We need the same Spirit that rested on the prophets to come alongside our expository sermons if we are to witness true change.

How Do You Access the Spirit's Power?

To be clear: No man can bridle, control, or obligate the Spirit of God. We *can* attempt to create an environment in which He enjoys operating. How do we do that? For starters, try these three things:

1. Proclaim the Scripture with accuracy. The Holy Spirit wrote Holy Scripture. Peter stated, "For no prophecy was ever produced by the will of man, but men spoke from God as they were carried along by the Holy Spirit" (2 Pet 2:21). The Holy Spirit is most likely to imbibe our expository sermons with His power when we accurately and honestly represent His single meaning. That is why we spent so much time talking about getting the verbal meaning right.

2. Spend time alone in His presence. The Apostle John said, "But as His anointing teaches you about everything, and is true, and is no lie—just as it has taught you, abide in Him" (1 Jn 2:27). Spend meaningful time with God. Sit alone with Him. Walk

with Him. Listen to Him. Alone time is often when He imparts wisdom—if we simply will slow down enough to listen. We've found that preachers often carve-out time for sermon prep, but few carve-out time to pray and listen. One wise old preacher once told me, "Everybody is in a hurry these days. About the time we normally finish praying—that is the time, when God is just beginning to open up His will." I think he's probably right. Spend more alone-time with Him.

3. Cover everything in prayer. Sometimes you can execute the perfect sermon, and it falls flat because it is not covered in prayer. You will feel awful because you know you didn't prepare spiritually in prayer. Conversely, sometimes you can preach a poor sermon, and it will stir men's hearts precisely because it "is" covered in prayer. You still will feel awful because you know you didn't prepare the sermon properly. Yet, there is no greater feeling in the world than when you have a fire in your bones, you prepare a rock-solid exposition from Holy Scripture, you spend quality time communing with the Lord about that message, you cover that message in passionate prayer, and you deliver that message in the demonstration of the Spirit and power! You will see before your very eyes: the Spirit of God touch men's hearts,

open their eyes, impart spiritual life to their dead souls, and transform their life, their family, and whole congregations! You will sleep well on those nights, and you should. For you will have accurately represented the King's message, with the King's blessing. You will sleep soundly while His Word and His Spirit do the rest!

Closing Thought

I must add one more important point. God's messengers must live pure and holy lives. If you are living in sin, then that is a sure-fire way to lose the Spirit's power on your life. You can preach wonderful sermons and spend time in passionate prayer, yet not have the Spirit's power on your life because He sees through your hypocrisy. Do the right things, for the right reasons, in the right spirit, and you will create a welcoming environment in which the Holy Spirit might be pleased to operate.

39

Things (on Preaching) They Didn't Tell Me in Seminary

Over twenty-five years of gospel ministry have come and gone for me. You learn many wonderful things along the way. I have served in our Lord's Kingdom in a lay capacity, a bi-vocational capacity, and a full-time capacity. You never stop learning, but you pick up helpful tidbits along the way. I'd like to share a few with you.

To Whom Much is Given, Much Will Be Required

Jesus told the parable of a faithful servant and an unfaithful servant. He concludes by saying, "Everyone to whom much was given, much will be required" (Luke 12:48b). Once you have been given an understanding of proper hermeneutics and homiletics, much is required. I apologize in advance for making your life more difficult, but you will thank me in the eternal state! Hopefully, the following tips will make things easier for you.

Things No One Told Me in Seminary

First, I once heard Alistair Begg interviewed on sermon preparation. He said his approach to sermon preparation goes something like this. After reading the preaching-text:

1. Think yourself empty.
2. Read yourself full.
3. Write yourself clear.
4. Pray yourself hot.
5. Be yourself always.

This is a good framework. Don't reverse #1 and #2. Always read the text first, then the commentaries. Otherwise, the commentaries might unduly influence your interpretation of the biblical author's intent.

Second, prepare three months of full manuscripts as soon as possible. An older, wiser preacher implored me once to do this. I didn't know why he was so insistent, but I did it nonetheless. It has been a lifesaver for a number of reasons.

Things (on Preaching) They Didn't Tell Me in Seminary

- One, emergencies happen: funerals, accidents, emergencies, etc. When they do, you already are (more or less) prepared for the next message.

- Two, difficult passages arise. It helps to have a longer period of time to think through difficult passages (illustrations will come along the way as well).

- Three, personal edification occurs. God will use your own sermons to convict or encourage you. I rarely remember exactly what I prepared three months ago. When I pull it out to review on the week I am to preach it, it sanctifies my heart all over again. This allows you, in a very real sense, to be impacted by the message yourself—before you preach it to others.

- Four, edits and adjustments sharpen the message. I modify, edit, or adjust the application early in the week. Circumstances will have changed from the time I wrote it (three months prior). The meaning of the passage remains fixed, but the specifica application may shift depending on circumstances.

Third, write-out full manuscripts. This isn't for everyone, I understand, but if you can get into the habit of it, it will sharpen your delivery. I use fourteen-point font, single space, and try to keep it less than five pages. That allows me room to depart from the manuscript extemporaneously. I (almost) always take the manuscript to the pulpit even though I don't need it. It keeps me on track if I begin to stray away from the preaching text.

Fourth, establish a routine. Routines can be a helpful discipline and save you much time. Currently, my off-day is Mondays. On Monday morning, I begin reviewing my sermon manuscript (which I prepared three months prior). I read it, edit it, and save it. I let it simmer throughout the week. Early on the Lord's Day morning, I read and pray through it at least twice. By most Sundays, I have internalized it by the time I step into the pulpit. Sometimes, during the sermon event, the Spirit takes me away from the exact words I wrote down. That doesn't bother me. I don't want to be tied to the manuscript. By following this deliberate preparation process, though, I generally have a comfortable command both (1) of the text itself and (2) the shape and flow of the message.

Finally, know when to stop the sermon. Closing a sermon is an art in itself. Few devote time to thinking how to close it. Be mindful of your audience. Your message is the most important thing they will experience all week, but many of them don't know that. I have had occasions where the time got away from me. Don't be afraid to stop abruptly and say something like, "Well, I have so much more to say, but we'll save it for another time." Most everyone will appreciate your honesty. No one has ever complained about that, either! Pastoral preaching is a long-term endeavor. Unless Jesus comes back, you always have next week.

Closing Thought

Each person has their own way. Make your preparations your own. If you follow my model, you should never feel stressed for time. You won't feel the pressure that "Oh, no! Sunday's coming!" Rather, you can't wait for Sunday to get here because the work has been done already. You will be able to worship and enjoy the experience along with everyone else. There is no greater joy than that!

www.ingramcontent.com/pod-product-compliance
Lightning Source LLC
Chambersburg PA
CBHW060832190426
43197CB00039B/2563